SAGE was founded in 1965 by Sara Miller McCune to support the dissemination of usable knowledge by publishing innovative and high-quality research and teaching content. Today, we publish over 900 journals, including those of more than 400 learned societies, more than 800 new books per year, and a growing range of library products including archives, data, case studies, reports, and video. SAGE remains majority-owned by our founder, and after Sara's lifetime will become owned by a charitable trust that secures our continued independence.

Los Angeles | London | New Delhi | Singapore | Washington DC | Melbourne

Advance Praise

A master of social welfare, social work and comparative social policy has written a masterful book. Enough already of professional social work, it has denounced itself with decades of foolish accommodations, empty scholarship and even a wandering commitment to those in need. Unique in these sorts of analyses, Mohan asks for the consideration of elements outside of the ambience of social work but with a humane and humanistic commitment. Reflecting the modesty of his deep learning, he refrains from offering a vision. These sorts of things, following Huxley, in their reduction of complexity only produce dynasties of tyranny. Perhaps Mohan's desire to 'demystify the power of materialism at the expense of philosophical streams' is best realized by first addressing the problems of social and economic inequality—two policies that are impeded by contemporary social work practice.

— **William M. Epstein**
Professor, Social Work
University of Nevada, USA

The Future of Social Work is a brilliant exposé of social work's ontology and authenticity—a subject mostly untouched by intellectuals in the field. Brij Mohan re-examines the Legitimacy Crisis of his calling with courage and convictions strengthened only by his vast knowledge and experiences. The 'heretic' thrust of this unmatched opus may save social work from falling into the traps of competitive, market-based professionalization. Uberization of social services, as the author calls, is imminent unless professionals overcome their myopic and siloed view of their practices. *The Future of Social Work* calls for a return to the core values and principles of human-centred social practice, against dehumanizing patronizing practice, by adhering to the seven algorithms: mission, education, service, empathetic humility, liberatory assistance, transparent effectiveness and buoyance.

— **Philip Young P. Hong**
Director, Center for Research on Self-Sufficiency
School of Social Work, Loyola University Chicago, USA

In *The Future of Social Work,* Professor Brij Mohan explores 'plateaus of practice' that believers might find unsettling. The book is a futuristic humane critique of contemporary professional ethics and practice. Mohan's 'Seven Pillars of Practice' proffer a 'liberatory praxis' that snorkels the depths of knowledge in search of jewels of truth. As a philosopher of social hope, the author suggests a paradigm shift, thereby challenging social sciences and humanities to thwart the possibility of a dystopian future.

Artificial intelligence will fundamentally change the patterns of social interactionality. Sapiens make mistakes; computers don't. If human frailty can be reduced by techno-digital means, the delivery of social services can be mediated more efficiently without social agencies staffed by fallible workers. The future of self-driven cars is mainly based on this premise. Brij Mohan contends that designing obsolescence is crucial for progress.

Students, educators and policy makers cannot ignore this seminal work by one of the most brilliant minds in academic discourse.

— **Sonia Kapur**
Assistant Professor, International Studies
University of North Carolina at Asheville, USA

The book is a scholarly analysis of social work education with an implicit comparative view. It also is a brutally honest critique of robotic–human interface. It posits social work in this conflict as slowly morphing into inanity.

Artificial Intelligence (AI) has changed much of transactional and operational services that fulfil human needs. Social services can't escape the avalanche of IT. Now, our profession has two choices: either get devolved into non-existence or launch a movement as defined by the author's theory of 'Seven Pillars of Practice'. Brij Mohan proffers seven transformational 'algorithms' which mainly include mission, education and service embedded in empathetic humility, authenticity and praxis—all achieving buoyancy above the sea of oppression.

A book like this has never been written before. I enthusiastically recommend this book for the future of social work.

— **Anil Navale**
Mentor, Masters in Social Work Programme
Navrachana University, India

The Future of
SOCIAL
WORK

The Future of
SOCIAL
WORK

Seven pillars of practice

BRIJ MOHAN

Los Angeles | London | New Delhi
Singapore | Washington DC | Melbourne

First published in 2018 by

SAGE Publications India Pvt Ltd
B1/I-1 Mohan Cooperative Industrial Area
Mathura Road, New Delhi 110 044, India
www.sagepub.in

SAGE Publications Inc
2455 Teller Road
Thousand Oaks, California 91320, USA

SAGE Publications Ltd
1 Oliver's Yard, 55 City Road
London EC1Y 1SP, United Kingdom

SAGE Publications Asia-Pacific Pte Ltd
3 Church Street
#10-04 Samsung Hub
Singapore 049483

Published by Vivek Mehra for SAGE Publications India Pvt Ltd, typeset in 10.5/13 pt Adobe Caslon Pro by Fidus Design Pvt. Ltd., Chandigarh and printed at Chaman Enterprises, New Delhi.

Library of Congress Cataloging-in-Publication Data
Name: Mohan, Brij, author.
Title: The future of social work: seven pillars of practice / Brij Mohan.
Description: Thousand Oaks: SAGE Publications India Pvt Ltd, [2018] |
   Includes bibliographical references and index.
Identifiers: LCCN 2018010274| ISBN 9789352806256 (print (hb): alk. paper) |
   ISBN 9789352806263 (e pub 2.0) | ISBN 9789352806270 (e book)
Subjects: LCSH: Social service.
Classification: LCC HV40. M556 2018 | DDC 361.3/2—dc23
LC record available at https://lccn.loc.gov/2018010274

ISBN: 978-93-528-0625-6 (HB)

SAGE Team: Amrita Dutta, Guneet Kaur, Shaonli Deb and Ritu Chopra

For

Prem

Thank you for choosing a SAGE product!
If you have any comment, observation or feedback,
I would like to personally hear from you.

Please write to me at **contactceo@sagepub.in**

Vivek Mehra, Managing Director and CEO, SAGE India.

Human beings are not wicked by nature.... We are hampered by the Paleolithic Curse: genetic adaptations that worked very well for millions of years of hunter-gatherer existence but are increasingly a hindrance in a globally urban and techno scientific society. We seem unable to stabilize either economic policies or the means of governance higher than the level of a village.
—Edward O. Wilson (2014: 176)

Out beyond ideas of wrongdoing and right doings,
There is a field. I will meet you there.
—Rumi, *Open Secrets*: 158: 8

[T]he earth, our home, is beginning to look more and more like an immense pile of filth.
—Pope Francis, *Laudato Si*

Contents

Foreword

One of the main reference points of modern systems theory is the presumption that systems always reproduce themselves by the very same mechanisms that characterize them as elementary closed systems; in other words, they permanently reproduce themselves by extending and elaborating those mechanisms from which they are made—and reproduction actually means that they also apply the ideas from which they are made, as means of repair, as means of overcoming inherent shortcomings. Obviously, this is a presumption that is not without problems, performing a bit against the notion brought forward by Einstein: we cannot find the solutions of our problems by applying those means that actually caused the problems.

Brij Mohan shows with his new book the deep truth of such stance by presenting his reflections about social work that lost ground and also ceiling, and even all the space between. In other words, he criticizes a conception that lost a clear raison d'être, a formulated nomos and the breathing space within which practice is developed as part of ongoing social processes. Moreover, it even lost a relevant understanding of what the social is.

The one—and commonly walked—way of dealing with such challenge follows the rules of what is criticized. To take just one example, the claim of evidence-based practice is commonly criticized *by giving evidence of its failure.* Or new theories rebuke the old ones, while still *referring to the same ontological and epistemological frameworks.* Indeed, as we read on page 39, 'The age of reason has fuelled the engines of anger. The complexity of social issues is challenging'.

In this light, Mohan's proposal for a social practice as a 'discursive idea of transformative practice' is itself a discursive process, the author entering into a discourse: with himself, relevant institutions and the practice itself.

This already marks a fundamental paradigmatic challenge as one of the central critiques put forward by the author is the shortcoming of social work, increasingly geared towards a narrowed understanding of individuals acting in a social space, while this space itself is hollowed out. As much as this is an issue of and for the profession, it can only be understood in the wider context of society in which

> [w]ork as invented by our civilization will morph into apps. 'Social' as a qualifying prefix will become redundant as social institutions continue to meltdown. Simple algorithms will wipe out all the tasks, skills and checklists that therapists and social service workers employ with protective 'licenses'. No one likes an unlicensed neuro-surgeon; however, licensing as a means to exclude dissent amounts to censorship. [27]

This book provides a personal account of the author's experience, not suitable for apps, too cumbrous for digitalized text and document analysis and challenging a professional understanding of which the glue is an administration for which problems do only exist during office hours, as Hans Achinger contented a long time ago—'problems and suffering that occur outside of office hours are invidious'.[1] This personal account resists the paradox that '[h]umans evolve [while] developmentality will devolve compassion into a vocation; and departmentality will degrade disciplinarities under the cover of science. Techno-hubris will shape human needs and services as functionally designed by its own necessities'.

The book is a valuable and timely contribution as it provokes the reader: not another sober analysis adding to the many that already exist, but personal, emphatic resistance against a profession and training of professionals that reinvents the humanity by misdirecting social existence towards a planet of ice and the jeopardy of a cage for which the key is lost by the age of reason, in the very same way as it is captured in Goethe's *Faust* by the words:

---

[1] 'Leiden, die außerhalb der Dienstzeit auftreten, sind mißlich,. *(Achinger, Hans, 1953:Soziale Sicherheit. Eine historisch-soziologische Untersuchung neuer Hilfsmethoden; Stuttgart: 43).*

And furtive shift from place to place. To nonsense reason turns, and benefit to worry. Woe unto you that you're a grandchild, woe!

The challenge Brij Mohan takes up bravely is the one of accepting loneliness, paradoxically needed when aiming on resisting technocratically induced individualism. He shows that he rightfully can say, 'I consider myself to be a humanist and social scientist. Alas, I was lonely in this strife. Our school chose to become a part of College of Human Sciences and Education for very pragmatic reasons' [68 f]. We can only hope that people who read it—and many should—see this as well as a wake-up call. And as such it is a challenge for the reader, not necessarily agreeing with all details, meticulously elaborated, but acknowledging the fundamental result: that we face a suicide of professional action if we are not ready to accept the need to a fundamental change of our thinking—and practice.

Peter Herrmann
Availles-Limouzine
France

Prologue

*An eternal truth is a dead truth that has returned to the In-itself.
A truth has not* become; *it is becoming [devenante]. And at the
end of its becoming, it dies. That does not mean that it becomes
false. It becomes* indeterminate, *that is we longer grasp it in its
context and with its articulations but as a bone with which one
constitutes a new organism. … The foundation of truth is freedom.
This non-truth is ignorance or lie.*
—Jean-Paul Sartre (1992: 12–13).

Human fallibility drives survivalist engines to become civilized. But our frailty fails us. What Edward Wilson calls *Paleolithic Curse* is essentially our species' dysfunctional (2014: 177) adaption to a new brave world. 'People find it hard to care about other people beyond their own tribe or country, and even then past one or two generations' (Wilson 2014: 177).

The duality of past and future is only compounded by a brief history of time. Relativity, reductionism and romanticism change our perception of social reality. Yuval N. Harari's intriguing new book *Homo Deus* (2017) does not solve any human problems. Earlier in *Sapiens* (2015), Harari asked a simple question: Can we ever free our behaviour from the legacy of our ancestors? Robert Gordon's *Rise and Fall of American Growth* (2016) alerts us of hard times ahead. History's most nagging question remains unanswered: Can we as a human race survive our own trappings? Pankaj Mishra's *Age of Anger*, likewise, unravels the history of the present. Mishra's diagnosis goes back to the Enlightenment, specifically Nietzschean 'ressentiment'. Enlightenment thinkers sought to liberate humans from the constraints of religion and traditions to pursue their self-interests. These ideals, Mishra argues, 'underpin the modern embrace of free-market capitalism, which took sole position on the world stage after the collapse of state socialism in 1989' (*Time* 2017, February 20: 20).

Enlightenment did predict populism. My plea for *Enlightenment II* (Pinker 2018) has long been to reinvent *homo sapiens* to ward off the dystopian reality predicted by Harari.

Human race has been subjected to utopian and dystopian visions of reality since long. From Thomas More (1965) to Karl Marx (1913) to Sigmund Freud (1961), one perpetually strives for hope amidst despair.

There is no winter of despair. But this is not exactly the spring of hope. This post-Dickensian paradox is the metaphor for contemporary human conditions. This monograph is a search for transformative pathways that improve the human condition in troubled times. This benign, simple formulation sits at the heart of what is intellectually named a sociology of knowledge. While I remain indebted to this field, I seek to go beyond its disciplinarity. In my quest for social practice (SP) as a discipline, I deal with the realms of social reality that is 'socially' constructed for the future of human race.

The trajectory of this thought is not easily discernible without implicit ideological predilections. I believe in scientific revolution (Kuhn [1962]1996). Science in and of itself is a neutral force. The alchemy of human and social reality morphs science into a messiah or a devil. The main—perhaps the only—challenge that humanity confronts is posed by *Homo Deus*. Yuval Noah Harari, an Israeli world historian, aims 'to upgrade humans into gods and turn *Homo Sapiens* into *Homo Deus*' (2017). *Sapiens* (Harari 2005), who invented the hydrogen bomb, cannot deinvent it.

Social work's (SW's) future, like the future of 'work' itself, is uncertain. All work is 'social'. SW's inner contradictions further call for serious discussion since human needs, social issues and public 'will' will morph in congruence with societal evolution in the digital age. This is a formidable spectre.

The decline or 'retreat', as Edward Luce (2017) contends, of Western liberalism is unsettling. Luce argues that the Western values that organized a democratic order are now under mortal threat. Canada's public policies have contributed to its sustained peace and prosperity. However, social interventions, public policies and social services do not always shape social reality; they simply sustain a repaired unit to function more effectively. This ameliorative, restorative, medical and psychological approach to human imperfections is fraught with fallacies of change, a kind of social change that does not 'help'.

SW is a benign, quasi-professional approach to problem-solving, a formidable process over which practitioners of change—or therapists of misdiagnosed maladies—have little control. Agency-embedded roles, tasks and learning experiences offer controlled circumstances to operate. The reality stands out in the field like an elephant in a conference room. SP, on the other hand, is beyond the constraints imposed by *logos* and its 'departmental' culture. I use SW and SP interchangeably with the nuanced implicitness of distinct ethos.

Darkness at noon is disappointing. It can be challenging as well. 1958: It was dawn before darkness in Mussoorie when I ran into R.N. Saxena, Founding Director, Institute of Social Sciences (ISS), Agra, that I later joined for pursuing master of social work (MSW). My examination scores were highest in a cohort of 75+ graduates but I received near pass marks (105/200) in the so-called fieldwork. ISS, as I learnt, was an excellent extension of Lucknow University's social sciences since most of my professors spilled over from there. A fresh doctor of social work (DSW) from Columbia University and a protégé of the famed Evelyn M. Burns, named S. Zafar Hasan, was building a doctoral programme in SW under the leadership of Radha Kamal Mukherjee, India's 'father of sociology'. I left Agra in despair and joined Lucknow University to obtain PhD in SW (1964). I taught SW there for 13 years; 1 March 1975, I left India and emigrated to the United States with an illusion that SW might transform the world.

On a sultry, humid southern morning in April 1984, I was hospitalized in a critical condition. A month after a major abdominal surgery, when I returned to work—three weeks before the recommended convalescence—I sensed a hideous unease. The pressure of transformational work—mainly pertaining to the incorporation of Louisiana State University School of Social Work into the Graduate School and initial preparation for a proposal for doctoral programme in SW, mainly faculty recruitment, promotion and tenure processes—nearly consumed me. However, the outcome was so sweet and substantial that the School of Social Work (henceforth referred to as the school) continues to thrive on accomplishments.

I had resigned from deanship in July 1986 to establish my eligibility for a promised Boyd Professorship (university's highest reward for 'international' recognition). The three decades that followed gave me an opportunity to grasp how organizational goal-displacement thrives at the expense of creativity.

This book is a very small, humble tribute to the people—mostly my students, family and teachers—who kept me going. Since I bear, with great honour and pride, an Indo-American (not Asian American!) identity badge, my deliberate efforts to make this book a worthwhile read to those who work in the 'trenches' to achieve peace and justice is a reward in itself. I make suitable, albeit short, comparative–analytic references to contextualize the ordeal of two great democracies. I added Chapter 9 to proffer an integrated view of my work in a rather nutshell. It was not an easy task; I got some ideas and help from certain friends whose encouragement has been inspirational. Shortcomings are solely mine.

Alienated and estranged, I used my adversity to my advantage. I taught with love and wrote with vengeance, becoming a better teacher and renowned author. I saw how responsibility was the shortest, albeit hardest, cut to freedom. It was the toughest patch to transform the poison of angst and anger into self-empowerment.

I retired 25 December 2009, having served the Louisiana State University (LSU) for 34 years. This monograph is an oeuvre of my work during the last three decades of my post-dean years at LSU. The pages that follow unravel certain concepts, conflicts and contradictions that embody SW's contemporary culture and its influence on people who serve it. Opinions and views may vary depending on individuals' interests and affiliations. Nevertheless, factuality sustains itself.

Social institutions nurture and serve society in vital fields of life. The spectre of meltdowns of these institutions cannot be overlooked when we offer 'problem-solving' skills in a rather discordant manner.

The obsolescence of methods, skills and values in a transient culture is a sign of entropy. This book seeks to offer critical insights as a simple pathway on the cusp of change that belies reason. 'Postmodernism is an instrument of power', claims Noam Chomsky. He is right. Postmodernity's instruments of power—inclusion, diversity, political correctness and other non-essentialist attributes of deconstruction—failed Derrida and Rorty. My profession has used this power less professionally than any other academic field I know of.

I wasn't born an American; I became one. This odyssey is a formidable story. My work is a product of this compelling journey.

I am very grateful to SAGE for their interest in and support for my work. I am deeply touched by the professionalism of the entire SAGE team for helping me to improve the quality of this work. Professor (Dr) Peter Herrmann's kind Foreword is deeply appreciated. I shared this manuscript with a selected group of academics who know the subject. Some of their comments are posted on the back cover. Their reviews and suggestions have been most commendable.

I dedicate this work to Prem—my wife—who stood by me like a rock for over half a century with undying love, trust and support. My children, Anu and Sanjay, and grandchildren, Gujri, Quince and Aneel, are owed the strength that is required to write a book at 78.

Brij Mohan
Baton Rouge
Louisiana, USA

CHAPTER 1

Poverty, War and Welfare

The relationship between checks and balances on the one hand and reliance on the rule of reason on the other is the Da Vinci Code of American democracy.
—Al Gore (2007: 215).

Human acquisitiveness and pugnacity must have been pivotal in waging wars. The reasons of war have not changed much ever since territoriality manifested itself as a primary motivation for human strife. Ideologies and their rationalized versions played havoc with people who lost battles and belongings. The origins of slavery, inequality and poverty perhaps lie deep in human psyche. Structural–environmental forces might have driven the innate demons to wider and deeper control and power to institutionalize the inequality as the basis of hierarchized social organization.

Hegemonies of power developed a culture of control and exploitation which perpetuated poverty. War thus became an instrument of powerful control. Since times immemorial, a sense of benevolence has manifested itself in forms of charity, altruism and philanthropy. Variants of such practices eventually constituted the foundation of residual social and public welfare.

This chapter is an overview of the main focus of this book: social welfare. There was a welfare system before social work (SW) became a profession and social policy assumed its own identity. The discussion presented here has two objectives: First, it offers a preliminary critique to students and readers who do not understand the complex relationship of charity and philanthropy with social problems, especially inequality and poverty. Second, more importantly, an analytical examination of war and welfare is presented to signify the dynamics of human frailties and social issues. In other words, there is a human element involved in human–social miseries. Eradication of poverty and social misery is an outcome of people's inability and failure to confront cultural–structural forces that cause misery, misfortunes and unhappiness in life. Ignorance of the facts reinforced by culturally classified dogmas perpetuate social problems as undiagnosed or ill-treated cancer that annihilates life.

The purpose of science and reason is to annihilate superstitions and beliefs that are dehumanizing. Science is not an accumulation of fancy instruments and collection of data subjected to sophisticated scopes and labs. It is a way of thinking clearly. Our sociocultural myopia is as dangerous as endemic plague.

There is a systemic linkage between the negative forces that cause misery and suffering. This is a 'negative' entropy not unlike the expanded chaos.

Inequality, Fundamentalism and War

The truth is what makes possible to exclude; to separate what is dangerously mixed; to distribute the inside and outside properly; to trace the boundaries between what is pure and what is impure.... The truth henceforth forms part of the great juridical, religious, and moral rituals required by the city. A city without truth is a threatened city. Threatened by mixtures, impurities, unfulfilled exclusions. The city needs the truth as a principle of division. It needs discourses of truth as it needs those who maintain the divisions.
—Michel Foucault, 17 March 1971 (2011: 187).

Fundamentalism, one of the main founts of fatal dissonance, is not a new evil. My guess is that it became more prevalent as religion and its rituals became better organised. According to Jeff Sharlet, fundamentalism is a 'movement that recasts theology in the language of empire'. This movement has avant-garde believers who 'call themselves the Family, or the Fellowship, and they consider themselves a core of men responsible for changing the world' (2008: 3). Sharlet writes:

> In contemporary America—from Cold War to the Iraq War, the period of the current incarnation's ascendancy—that means a culture remade in the image of a Jesus strong but tender, a warrior who hates the carnage he must cause, a man-god ordinary men will follow as he conquers the world in order to conform it to his angry love. These are the days of the sword, literally—wealthy members of the movement gift one another with real blades crafted to battle standards, a fad inspired by a Christian bestseller called *Wild at Heart: Discovering the Secret of a Man's Soul.* As a jargon, then, Maximalism isn't bad, but I think fundamentalism still strikes closest to the movement's desire for a story that never changes, a story to redeem all that seems random, a rock upon which history can rise. (2008: 4–5)

In the wake of a presidential campaign introducing Rick Stantorum, a church pastor named Dennis Terry delivered a 'stem-winder of a sermon':

> This nation was founded as a Christian nation. If you don't like the way we do things, I've one thing to say: Get Out! We don't worship Buddha. We don't worship Muhammad. We don't worship Allah. We worship God. We worship God's son Jesus Christ.
>
> (*Time* 2012, April 2)

A few years ago French economist Thomas Picketty in his classic opus on inequality (2014) resuscitated Karl Marx. He also emphasized the limits of social sciences. He wrote: 'The social sciences collectively known too little to waste time on foolish disciplinary squabbles' (2014: 334–34). There is an evolutionary streak in his revolutionary thesis. Picketty succinctly sums it up: 'The past devours the future' (2014: 571). In his copious theory, *r>g* is 'the central contradiction of capitalism' (571). In other words: 'The inequality *r>g* implies that wealth accumulated in the past grows rapidly than output and wages' (2014: 571). He explains:

> The inequality *r>g*, combined with inequality of returns on capital as a function of initial wealth, can lead to excessive and lasting concentration of capital: no matter how justified inequalities of wealth may be initially, fortunes can grow and perpetuate themselves beyond all reasonable limits and beyond any possible rational justification in terms of social utility. (214: 443)

In sum, the 'globalized patrimonial capitalism' (Picketty 2014: 573) and inequality will continue to coexist. I seriously doubt the effectiveness and possibility of the well-intended global 'progressive annual tax of capital' to combat inequality. Religious, political, cultural and military intuitions will perpetuate the evil structure of inequality. Education, free enterprise, welfare and corrupt public policies will recreate a dystopia of hopelessness amidst the rise of billionaires. Put simply, we socialize public miseries and allow the Wall Street to capitalize on human misfortunes.

Paroxysm of Populism

Kurt Andersen writes a damning history of the white Europeans', especially the puritan Protestants', quest for a private utopia in *Fantasyland: How America Went Haywire: A 500-Year History* (2017). Gold became a chimera. The gold-seekers today have become gravediggers in a global culture, as counter-factual fantasies have demolished the bar between reality and falsehood. We all dwell sometimes in *twilights of irrationalities*. But the problem assumes a monstrous character when the unbelievable becomes the norm. Andersen writes:

> What's problematic is going overboard, letting the subjective override objective, people thinking and acting as if opinions and feelings were just true as facts. The American experiment, the

original embodiment of the great Enlightenment idea of intellectual freedom, every individual free to believe anything she wishes, has metastasized out of control. From the start, our ultra-individualism was attached to epic dreams, sometimes epic fantasies—every American one of God's chosen people building a custom-made utopia, each of us free to reinvent himself by imagination and will. In America those more exciting parts of the Enlightenment idea have swamped the sober, rational, empirical parts. (2017: 5)

SW is a by-product of dreams and delusions. Social engineers and self-righteous altruists invented a pseudo-profession to hide the wounds of poverty and war with a subconscious guilt under the cover of philanthropy masquerading as professional help. As we will notice, a great civil society lost its innocence without resolving its adolescent complexes.

This is 2018: Mr Donald Trump is in the White House. By all accounts, his administration remains unabashedly anti-immigrants, especially from certain countries. Islamophobia and anti-brown policies and programmes are reflected in day-to-day incidents, tweets and social media with un-American messages. What has gone so wrong? Bruce Cannon Gibney, a columnist, indicts the current generation of boomers who 'destroyed everything'. Gibney said:

> Deplorables, deportables, economic malaise, rural resentment, coastal hauteur whatever—these are just symptoms. The root illness remains undiagnosed, but here it is: the baby boomers, that vast generation of Americans born in the first two decades after World War II. The body politic rests on the slab because boomers put it there, because decades of boomerism produced the problems and disaffection of which 2016 was merely the latest expression.
>
> (Gibney 2017)

An autopsy of American presidential election held in November 2016 reveals a brutal fact: Alienated, blue-collar, poor white Americans brought a man to power who spoke their language in pure nativist spirit. Mexican immigrants are 'rapists'; Muslims are 'terrorists'.

Return of the *Hilly Billy* is not an accidental episode in the American drama. In a book entitled *White Trash*, historian Nancy

Isenberg, the famed author of *Fallen Founder*, masterfully brings out 'The 400-year untold history of class in America' (2016). Isenberg contends:

> The poor, the waste, the rubbish, as they are variously labeled, have stood front and center during America's most formative political contests. During colonial settlement, they were useful pawns as well as rebellious troublemakers, a pattern that persisted amid class migration and landless squatters westward across the continent. Southern poor whites figured prominently in the rise of Abraham Lincoln's Republican Party, and in the atmosphere of distrust that caused bad blood to percolate among the poorer classes within the Confederacy during the Civil War. White trash were dangerous outliers in efforts to rebuild the Union during Reconstruction; and in the first two decades of the twentieth century, when the eugenics movement flourished, they were the class of degenerates targeted for sterilization. On the flip side, poor whites were beneficiaries of rehabilitative efforts during the New deal in LBJ's 'Great Society'. (Isenberg 2016: xv)[1]

Hillary Clinton had used the words 'basket of deplorables' for her opponents' supporters. American anxiety, avarice and atavism existed even prior to *the birth of a nation*. Gunnar Myrdal famously wrote that American creed is good but its practice is unjust and unfair. Hillary Clinton expressed 'regret' for comments in which she said 'half' of her rival's supporters are 'deplorable', meaning people who are racist, sexist, homophobic or xenophobic.[2] 'Post-truth' reality is an antithesis of 'post-material praxis' that I wrote about earlier (Mohan 1992):[3]

---

[1] I gratefully acknowledge Professor Isenberg's permission to comment on her brilliantly written history of an oft-neglected issue in America.

[2] http://www.cnn.com/2016/09/09/politics/hillary-clinton-donald-trump-basket-of-deplorables/ (accessed on 4 October 2016).

[3] '[T]he term was first used by David Roberts, then a blogger on an environmentalist website, Grist—as a modish myth invented by *de-haut-en-bas* liberals and sore losers ignorant of how dirty a business politics has always been' (*The Economist*, 10 September 2016); *The Economist* is tempted 'to dismiss the idea of "post-truth" political discourse'. I emphasized the nexus of 'post-material

The 'post-truth' society has produced a compound of two sets of *new revolutionaries*: We have known about the 'white trash' for about 400 years. The 'deplorable' represent the new Hillbillies left out by the ravages of globalized economy; 'basement dwellers' are reluctant liberals unable to confront the new realities of a hopelessly divided nation. And the millennial 'socialists'! The underlying commonality between the two is the perversion of a perpetual class war ingrained in the DNA of our society. How ironic is it that Donald Trump and Bernard Sanders, on the right and the left, became the champions of the poor, victims of a 'rigged *economy*'?[4]

American social scientists, in general, have downplayed the role of class in critiquing stratification of society. Race, gender, and lately LGBT, issues have dominated discourses on the human condition. When Patrick Moynihan characterized the black family as a flawed institution, he was basically 'blaming the victim'. No wonder, *Blaming the Victim* and *Culture of Poverty* have shaped much of public and social discourse in America.[5] Since other countries, by and large, look up for American innovations and ideas, the impact of these two pernicious views can be overlooked only at the expense of truth.

History though always written by victors always unravels truth and untruth. Nancy Isenberg's *White Trash* unfolds this reality beyond the ideological fog and conundrums of time. Erick Fonner's work has tremendously impressed me. I make no pretense to be a historian but I have great respect for history. In *Development, Poverty of Culture*

---

values' and social praxis—social media was not dominant at that time—in a world ravaged by euphemisms of falsehood.

[4] Donald Trump exploited the sentiments of poor white Americans who felt left out. Trump blamed the Mexicans and immigrants for their misery. Bernard Sanders accused the economy which is manipulated by Wall Street elites.

[5] This has been my contention that two sociological theories—'blaming the victim' and 'culture of poverty'—have shaped much of American social welfare policy. Even Patrick Moynihan blamed the 'black family' for 'the tangle of pathologies'. http://www.theadvocate.com/baton_rouge/opinion/letters/article_cb562958-4872-11e6-8b20-773e1328a95d.html?utm_medium=social&utm_source=facebook&utm_campaign=user-share (accessed on 1 December 2017).

and Social Policy, I made a modest attempt to demystify the inconvenient sociology of a welfare system[6] (Mohan 2011). Alvin Gouldner succinctly observed:

> The old society maintains itself also through theories and ideologies that establish its hegemony over the minds of men. Who therefore do not merely bite their tongues but submit to it willingly. It will be impossible either to emancipate men from the old society or to build a new one, without beginning, here and now, the construction of a total counter-culture, including new social theories; and it is impossible to do this without a critique of the social theories dominant today. (1971: 5)

The politics of social theory is fraught with conflicts. Critical social theory, Russell Keat argues,

> differs significantly both from the positivistic conception of social science, and from the main historical alternative to this, the hermeneutic or interpretive tradition.... Scientific knowledge, positivistically conceived, is inherently repressive, and contributes to the maintenance of a form of society in which science is one of the resources employed for the domination of one class by another, and in which the possibilities for a radical transformation towards a more rational society are blocked and concealed. (1981: 1–2)

Human evolution is a history of strife, survival and conquest. Post-industrial societies with emphasis on production, profit and scientific advancements did succeed in raising material resources but could not resolve let alone annihilate poverty and inequality. No wonder open-market economies created Silicon Valleys and transformed feudal–colonial systems into flourishing economies (India and China) without annihilating the scourges of inequality. This paradoxical state

---

[6] Arguing against the 'culture of poverty' school, I wrote about the 'poverty of culture' that perpetuates social misery and poverty.

of development implies that quest for equality is a romantic fallacy since poverty persists despite growth.

Sex, food and war have been constants in the dynamics of human–societal evolution. There was no slavery in caves. Primitive innocence, if it ever existed, did not last long. As soon as property and agriculture were invented, Rousseauean innocence vanished. It seems hard not to recognize the inherent–cultural–wiring mechanisms that perpetuate inequality and injustice. The emphasis here is on *invincible environmental imperatives*—genesis of 'class' rather than Darwinian determinism.

From terrorism to street violence, corporate rapaciousness to domestic brutality and casteism to classism, one finds the imprints of an incomplete *homo sapiens* masquerading as a civilized global citizen. Malcolm Potts and his co-author Thomas Hayden scientifically bring home the duality of 'biology of war and peace' (2008).

> The world is very clearly divided into 'haves' and 'have-nots'. About one billion people live on less than one dollar a day, while the richest 20 percent of the global population earn three quarters of the global income. In 2007, the two wealthiest individuals in the world had more money than combined GDP of the 45 poorest countries. The terrorists who have attacked the West, and who no doubt will do again, act largely because they live in a world of frustrated dreams. Their fundamentalist interpretations of religion and radical political philosophies offer an illusion of hope. Any of us might be attracted to such a perspective if we lived in the same environment. (2008: 354)

The Marxist vision of a classless society was shattered by the Stalins and Maos who championed the cause of their proletarian folks. Their surrogates have brought much pain and misery in the name of liberation. Gender and class injustices persist; global inequalities deep in. I seriously doubt if IBM's *Dr Watson* and 'cognitive computing' can ever wipe out this inhuman condition.

It is empowerment of women that still has promise to promote the cultural biology of peace. Objectification of women as a reality and metaphor will only reinvent a billionaire fascist who brags of groping women on way to the White House.[7,8]

Columnist George Will, quoting Nicholas Eberstad, concludes:

> Reversing social regression is more difficult than casing it. One manifestation of regression, Donald Trump, is perhaps perverse evidence that some of his army of angry men are at least healthily unhappy about the loss of meaning, self-esteem and masculinity that is a consequence of chosen and protracted idleness. (Will 2016: 7B)

Eberstad thinks policy innovations can reverse this 'social emasculation' which is unwelcome 'American Exceptionalism' (Eberstad 2016,[9] quoted by Will 2016).

Perverse regression is not a sudden event. Will believes in Oscar Lewis' *Culture of Poverty* (1961, 1965) that I refute. My thesis of *poverty of culture* is 'an argument against the prevailing orthodoxies and practices that partake in social sciences…. The poor, marginalized, underdeveloped peoples in the Global South present serious challenges to the credibility of globalization in the post-American World…' (Mohan 2011: xv).

Mass criminalization of marginalized groups is product of predatory chauvinism and its abominable manifestations. Modern penalty, in this age of terror, has become a new 'law and order' morality. The

---

[7] http://www.nytimes.com/2016/10/09/us/politics/donald-trump-campaign. html?emc=edit_th_20161009&nl=todaysheadlines&nlid=72603810 (accessed 9 October, 2016).

[8] The second presidential debate, 9 October 2016, was dark and vulgar; it set the new low in cultural swamps of American politics. See, http://www.newyorker. com/news/news-desk/donald-trump-narcissist-creep-loser?mbid=nl_161010_ Daily&CNDID=40380448&spMailingID=9663054&spUserID=MTMzMT g0NzY3MTk5S0&spJobID=1020760310&spReportId=MTAyMDc2MDMx MAS2 (accessed on 11 October 2016).

[9] George Will is a reputed conservative columnist. In his column he has quoted N. Eberstad to validate his point. *See*, http://www.nationalreview.com/ article/440807/men-without-work-nicholas-ebersradts-new-book-examines-family-erosion (accessed on 9 October 2016).

state's monopoly over this exclusive authority has been challenged by the anti-state movements, embodied in Islamic State of Iraq and Syria (ISIS) and its offshoots. In the United States, far-right groups are no less aggressive. From tea-partiers and birthers to home-grown secessionists, the evilness of state is nihilistic anarchism which is always practised at the expense of powerless people. It puzzles me when I hear educated people in the United States praising Rodrigo Duterte's war on drugs—an extrajudicial killing spree—in Philippines.[10]

'We are witness not merely to the internationalization of class conflict but to the transformation of the structure of class,' writes Norman Birnbaum (1998: 38). The most enlightened view of evolutionary—not revolutionary!—class structure is summed up by Edward O. Wilson:

> The most complex forms of social organizations are made from high levels of cooperation. They are furthered with altruistic acts performed by at least some of the colony members. The highest level of cooperation and altruism is that of eusociality, in which some colony members surrender part or all of their personal reproduction in order to increase reproduction by the 'royal' caste specialized by that purpose. (2013: 61)

Eusociality may have transformed caste into class. The functional hierarchy of the production–ownership–distribution machine is actually an acceptance of the inbuilt inequality that creates both perceptual and organizational barriers amongst people. 'Your class determines how you look at your fellow creatures'.[11] A new class war masquerades in varied cultural forms and colours designed by divisive ideologies.

---

[10] 'The President was unapologetic about his grim campaign and its fallout. "Rich or poor, I do not give a sh-t." Duterte said at a recent press conference. "My order is to destroy"'. *Time*, 10 October 2016: 49.

[11] 'Dr. Dietze's and Knowles's own view is that the upper classes pay less attention because they believe random strangers have little to offer. Perhaps one way to test their hypothesis would be to return their experiment at a Buckingham Palace garden party' (*The Economist*, 15 October 2016: 76).

Religious fundamentalism and political correctness, in many ways, practise a populist penalty which borders on omnidisciplinarity that Michel Foucault brilliantly talked about. Foucault changed the way we ought to assess the promiscuous quality of our culture. In his classic *Discipline and Punish*, he describes the monastic model in reference to the discipline of workshop. 'The prison must be the microcosm of a perfect society in which individuals are isolated in their moral existence, but in which they come together in strict hierarchical framework, with no lateral relation, communication being possible in a vertical direction' (Foucault 1995: 238). In Pakistan, a nuclear power, honour killings and export of terror is not uncommon. In India, the world's largest democracy and an aspiring world power, a Dalit, usually a man, may be lynched for loving a high-caste man or woman. In the Middle East, 'amongst the believers', one never knows what happens to you if you are from the West. In the United States, you—a black man—are not safe should you be walking in a decent area. From Ferguson, MS to Baton Rouge, LA, we have seen the horrors of a divided nation. Americans prefer security at the expense of their creed. The duality of 1 per cent and 99 per cent is a callous reality.

No one could have imagined what Wells Fargo did to its clients.[12] It is interesting Wells Fargo generously supported *Social Work*'s 60th anniversary issue dealing with 'fiscal capability and asset development' to 'take up the challenge of advancing economic and social justice for all'. (*Social Work*, October 2016: 295) This Wall Street approach to achieving social and economic justice is the greatest fraud in the history of professional education. Instead of being a candle, social work has become a mirror of a corrupt system.[13]

'White trash', Isenberg succinctly points out, sustain the foundations of an unequal society. Note how the world's mightiest nation uses its people to maintain a rigged and rotten system:

[12] http://money.cnn.com/2016/09/20/investing/wells-fargo-elizabeth-warren-resign-criminal-investigation/index.html?iid=EL (accessed on 14 October 2016).

[13] My address to the 4th Congress of 'National Association of Professional Social Workers in India', 22 October 2016; https://vimeo.com/188037219 (accessed on 1 December 2017). This has been a central issue as critique of social work's nature and ideology.

Job opportunities for all—the myth of full employment—is just a myth. The economy cannot provide employment for every one.... Modern America's reserve army of the poor are drummed into the worst jobs, the worst-paid positions, and provide the labor force that works in coal mines, cleans toilets and barn stalls, picks and plucks in field as migrant laborers, or slaughter animals. Waste people remain the 'mudsills' who fill out the bottom layer of the labor pool on which society's wealth rests. *Poor whites are still taught to hate—not to hate those who are keeping them in line.* (2016: 315; emphasis mine)

Myths, misinformation and mendacity pervert truth. Higher education, which has commoditized values, knowledge and skills, itself looks like a slaughterhouse of ideals. Having lived in Louisiana for more than four decades, 'I found how low the higher ups go when they feel threatened by the rivals of "white trash"' (Mohan 2002: 122–159).[14]

It is ironic that society's 'wretched ones' should be the foundational protectors of their own perpetrators. It is more than Marxian 'false-consciousness'. What Vedic scholars called karma (action) and dharma (moral code), a destined cycle of life and death wrapped in a transmigratory journey, is actually an evolutionary process. Revolutions come and go. Each revolutionary epoch leaves behind collaterally damaged people. They sustain the 'chains' that enslave them. Perhaps, 'men fashion unfreedom as a bribe for self-perpetuation' (Becker 1975: 49). Norman Brown sums it up: 'If the emergence of social privilege marks the Fall of Man, the Fall took place not in the transition of from "primitive communism" to "private property" but in the transition from ape to man' (1959: 251).

Psychoanalytically viewed, 'white trash' is rooted in the American psyche. I am tempted to cite a few lines that portray the hidden violence in the tales of these 'white trash' people:

[14] Chapter IV, 'Sociology of Social Work: Historializing Truth' (122–159). The Dixie Land is famed for its 'Confederacy' culture. Louisiana is the epicenter of this traditional way of life. I experienced exclusion at work and in the community, at large.

[Robert] Byrd referred to people on welfare as 'fornicating deadbeats'.... Carter still had to run a 'redneck' campaign in order to win.... [James] Dickey reinvented himself as the child of hillbillies.... [His] novel published in 1970, was a tortured exploration of lost manhood, an attempt to recover his 'inner hillbilly'.... In this psychosexual thriller, the dandified city folk aren't merely given their comeuppance; they are forced to rediscover their primal instincts.... Dickey's story had its giant appeal because the search he described found expression elsewhere in American society. (Quoted from Isenberg 2016: 279–280)

The impact and influence of James Dickey's *Deliverance* has been phenomenal; its counter-culture–class war that we see today is return of the 'upscale rednecks' challenging the establishment with wish-fulfilling mantras of change. Racial injustice, inequality and poverty are scourges that sustain *class* as an inalienable condition. *Redneck Roots* are as American as its pie. No Trumpian revolution can transform it into Bernie Sanders' socialism. A creed without deed is a fanciful dream.

The United States of America is a divided nation. Race, gender and class continue to decivilize people. Columnist George Will, known for erudite conservative views, once raised a pertinent question. My response to his opinion has a contextual relevance:[15]

In reference to George Will's commentary on social science (July 7), I am impelled to offer a few comments in light of the rising tide of extremism, violence, and intolerance in our culture. Alton Sterling's unforgettable tragedy in our Baton Rouge community highlights my observations. 'Would this have happened if the driver were white?' asks a governor up north.

The columnist in reference has an ossified notion of family structure and social capital as misrepresented by dated sociologists like Coleman, Moynihan, and Murray. The Coleman report was a chilling indictment of the dysfunctional educational system that

---

[15] http://www.theadvocate.com/baton_rouge/opinion/letters/article_cb 562958-4872-11e6-8b20-773e1328a95d.html (Letter to the Editor, *The Advocate*, 13 July 2016; accessed on 10 August 2017).

bred inequality. Integrationists, however, were wronged when segregation was perpetuated at the expense of equality. Politicians on right and left never implemented the report's intended strategies. Moynihan's pernicious 'tangle of pathology' simply blamed the victim, which, regretfully, continues to reinforce much of social policy in our country. It's not the 'culture of poverty', sir, —it's the 'poverty of culture' (Mohan 2011a) that continues to sustain a 'bifurcated society' (Will's words) that incubates fallacies of civility. It's imperative that a new dynamic of race, gender and class is re-contextualized in the din of pervasive racial injustice, white privileges and political savagery.

Edward Luce, in his new book (2017), laments 'degeneration' of Western politics which is a matter of grave global concern. In *The Retreat of Western Liberalism*, Luce worries about liberal democracy and its future. He says that liberal democracy cannot be shored up without a 'clear-eyed grasp of what has gone wrong' (*The Economist*, 24 June 2017: 77).

Charles Murray, a divisive voice of the radical right, was lately protested at Middlebury College where Mr Murray's audience was disrupted by violent protest. His controversial views took an ominous turn as reported by *The Economist*:

> Their protests quickly escalated from jovial catcalling to prohibitive heckling and then—after Mr Murray was interviewed on camera by Alison Stanger, a Middlebury professor, in a separate room—into violence. Ms Stanger's hair was yanked; the car in which the pair departed was mobbed. 'I feared for my life', she subsequently wrote. (11 March 2017: 31)

The demise of academic freedom, regardless of the politics, is detrimental to democracy. Again, endorsing George Will regarding academic decay:[16]

---

[16] http://www.theadvocate.com/baton_rouge/opinion/letters/article_859d07e9-e8f6-5926-8a6d-1be193bb9e47.html (Letter to the Editor, 'Lamenting the Demise of Dissent on Campus,' *The Advocate* accessed on 10 August 2017).

Esteemed columnist George Will, whom I seldom endorse, has a point when he applauds Purdue University, especially its leadership, following Princeton and the Chicago policy affirming freedom of speech and search for truth in academia. Higher education is indeed a house in disarray. (*The Advocate*, 20 December 2015: 7B)

Reality principle that sustains search for knowledge cannot survive in a culture where education is commoditized based on pleasure—rather than reality—principle.

The demise of dissent is a new reality. A mindlessly hierarchized system corrupted by the Byzantine politics of arrogant athletic affluence, inbreeding, local privileges and perverted versions of political correctness has promoted mediocrity, nepotism, exclusionary practices and a devious system of rewards and recognition that callously alienates meritorious intellectuals with impunity.

How can you ever expect the Chicago policy to succeed when carpetbaggers, careerists, anti-intellectual narcissists sit at the helm of power in the temples of enlightenment and learning?

From 'Fire and Fury' to Rigveda's 'Aayudha' (Weapons of War)

The *New York Times* (2017) editorialized after the worst mass murder in the US history. The banality of mayhem unfolded as a man owning 49 guns sprayed thousands of bullets killing at least 59 people and injuring 527, when they were enjoying a country music festival in Las Vegas. A governor said, 'You cannot regulate evil'. 'Of all the ways in which American democracy is showing symptoms of turning into a dysfunctional state, the inability to face down the gun lobby is surely one of the most egregious', writes John Cassidy in *The New Yorker*.[17]

The gun culture and its advocates argue: Guns don't kill; people do. This perverse justification for gun ownership and its vulgar consequences directly benefit mental health industry. Every murderer

---

[17] https://www.newyorker.com/news/john-cassidy/las-vegas-gun-violence-and-the-failing-american-state (accessed on 3 October 2017).

is seen as a mental patient needing 'help' to prevent carnage. Thus goes the insane maxim. Steven Paddock, the Las Vegas shooter, suffered no mental illness. He had no drug and substance issue. He was a gambler. This makes it a case for mental health services. But how could a social worker help prevent this tragedy?

We as citizens of a civil society stand at the crossroads of war and peace, rhetoric and reality. Obscenities of hyper-democracy and fundamentalist soullessness of new totalitarianism have morphed civility into a dystopian barbarism.

Populist paroxysms brought Vietnam War followed by destruction of Iraq and Syria while Afghanistan, Sudan, Yemen and many Middle East nations painfully wallow in the ruins of hunger and war. From the hoary antiquity, humanity has gone through phases of near extinction, 'mantras of mayhem', and ritualized versions of slavery and servitude. The violence of freedom and unfreedom is a perpetual saga for equality and justice. I offer a few glimpses of perpetual injustice, like racism in America.

In a recent book *Ants Amongst Elephants*, author Sujatha Gidla (2017) recounts the plight of a Dalit family—an undying odyssey of an intergenerational 'untouchable' family from India to New York. This memoir 'chronicles her family's experience of the contest between modern India's civilizing aspirations and the savagery of a decaying but persistent old India' (*The Economist*, 29 July 2017: 72). Gidla's eloquence and unique biography should concern everyone who cares about equality in an unequal world:

> I still look forward to a day when there are no poor people in the world, and I agree with my uncle that it will take a revolution to achieve this. (2017: 305)

The persistence of 'untouchability'—the nadir of inequality—is like the persistence of poverty. By implication, it is the culture that perpetuates it. If poverty is the midwife, untouchability is womb that delivers children of injustice fathered by the perpetrators of a predatory culture. Nothing could be more cruel than the mythologized version of slavery that lives through the impermeable prison of subhuman destiny dictated by nefarious interpretations of karma and dharma.

The caste hierarchy is vulnerable to class. Class conflicts and modernity's contradictions have produced some fruitful results. Affirmative policies and practices in both the United States and India have demolished the vestiges of slavery and 'untouchability'. It is racism that trumps both 'gender' and 'class'. A brown Hindu millionaire in Chicago is still an unwanted person who invokes hideous slogans like 'Go home!'.

The caste model has been used by Western sociologists as a model of functional rationality. Parsons' theory of action is a bastardized version of karma. It maintains a system that yields results that are dear to the ruling elites.

A silent revolution occurred in the postcolonial India when a gifted 'untouchable' boy born in Madhya Pradesh caught the favourable attention of a feudal patron in Indore. Bhimrao Ambedkar became *Baba Sahib*, not unlike the Gandhi who became the *Mahatma*. B.R. Ambedkar, India's first Law Minster who chaired the Constitutional Assembly, deservedly became the liberator of millions of Harijans, now called Dalits. Ambedkar's praxis on 'Dalan (oppression) and Liberation' is appropriately situated in the textual context, especially when some Hindu fundamentalists seem to politicize his life, legacy and contributions.

Bhimrao Ambedkar is one of the main architects of Modern India. His crusade against the evils of 'untouchability' and caste system led to mass revolution that shook the foundation of established hegemonies of power. His political exclusion from the mainstream is now being challenged. To *dalitize* Ambedkar as merely a messiah of the 'untouchables' will be an error. Ambedkar's principled thoughts and actions elevated him to the status of a liberator of all oppressed people. I contextualize his work and legacy in the politico–historical background of India's democracy. I signify Ambedkar and his work as an exemplar in the realm of transformation. His conversion to Buddhism was a rebuke to the Brahmanic Vedic culture that institutionalized inequality.

As the 'Founder of Modern India', Ambedkar's relevant contributions seem to be threefold:

* Constitutional Provisions
* Champion of the downtrodden
* The Ambedkarian Praxis

At a juncture when social institutions are melting down and cults of terror, violence and crime are mushrooming all around, it is imperative that we pause for a moment and rethink the purpose of democracy, good government and the politics of meaningful change.

As long as helpless woman and dehumanized children continue to suffer, workers who produce wealth remain alienated and the marginalized folks remain hopeless and powerless, man-made misfortunes will continue to deepen the wounds of inequality. Thomas Piketty's take on capital (2014) has been central to my critique of post-industrial society.

Times have changed so dramatically. Buddhists in Myanmar are killing Muslims while *Bhima Sena* and *Gau Rakshaks* are playing violent games. Likewise, backlash against Mexicans and other immigrants in the United States is demeaning the ethos of democracy. In conclusion, equality and justice lead to common progress which translates into freedom. Oppression, that is, *dalan*, is an equal opportunity evil.

Patterns of politics and human behaviour are universally morbid and populist. The hoary antiquity of India's rituals is another comparative vantage point in evaluative focus. Rigveda, the oldest written scripture, unfolds the evolution of the Aryans' journey and their Vedic philosophy.

In his fascinating book (2014), Harsh Mahaan Cairae unfolds the 'mythology and violence'. It may be worthwhile to discern the roots of ritualized behaviours that sustain the contours of primordial psyche.

Ethnic evolution is a natural process and outcome of human–societal development. Human diversities and conflicts date back to a hoary past. As pre-agrarian societies began to settle, attachment to cattle, land and basic essentials of tribal life morphed into a new phenomenal institution named *property*. As Rousseau vividly conceptualized, rise of property is essentially the foundation of civil society.

Modern world is a macrocosmic extension of new tribalism. Imperatives of acquisitive–territorial proclivities posit varied peoples in a conflict-ridden world marked by the new gods of guns, gains and greed idealized by the myths of a past that does not exist. The present represents a culmination of both past and future that defines the culture of indigenous people in a complex whole new world.[18]

Asian indigenous character is essentially heterogeneous and conflict-ridden. In other words, there is nothing truly 'Asian' in Asia. This oxymoronic quality sets the stage for a kind of *Game of Thrones* continually played out in different theatres despite some historico–mythological commonalities.

A close examination of Buddhism, its origin and relationship with Vedanta and Aryan history unravels the trajectory of peoples, which represents a pantheon of indigenous nationalities. The history of human race and culture is shrouded in the labyrinths of time and space mythologized by prehistoric pundits of scriptures. Thousands of years ago, the Vedas were written in Sanskrit by *rishis* (sages) in the Himalayan hermitages. In quest of a certain universal truth and search for meanings of life and death, these men and women sought enlightenment. Holy scriptures reflect that metaphysical awakening.

While historical evidence is in abundance, no systemic record of cultural evolution is found. As famously said, *absence of evidence is not evidence of absence.* Myths, fantasies and legends are not history. History itself is an interpretation of events by humans. The discovery of Indus Valley civilization—more recently of Dwarika—is an evidence of a past laid buried under the unfathomable layers of time. As scholars

---

[18] It is in the context of 'Eurasia' that I posit this evolutionary trajectory of the Aryans of Asia. Eurasia implies: 'Eurasia covers around 55,000,000 sq. km (21,000,000 sq. mi), or around 36.2% of the Earth's total land area. The landmass contains around 5.0 billion people, equating to approximately 72% of the human population. Humans first settled in Eurasia between 60,000 and 125,000 years ago'. https://en.wikipedia.org/wiki/Eurasia (accessed on 31 August 2015).

and scientists unravelled facts, interpretations became reality. Sanskrit, a moribund classic imprint of immeasurable depth, is an embodiment of the remains of an ancient culture. Saraswati, India's prehistoric holy river, where sages meditated and wrote the hymns of wisdom is no more a mythical fiction.[19]

The mystic of Indo-Aryan culture—its poetic aesthetics, fore-knowledge of science (mathematics, Ayurveda, astrology, aeronautics) and artefacts—is shrouded in the mist of antiquity and mythology. Decoding, interpretation and analysis of Vedic literature mark Cairae's evidence-based account of their journey. Before colonially scripted Balkanization, India laid as a graveyard of one of the most advanced civilizations on this planet. The excavated ruins of a fallen people mock at the arrogance of modernity that has lost its evolutionary force. This book brings to fore the salience of history's forgotten lessons that can slow down, if not prevent, the dissolution.

Between the two polarities of religio-Aryan faith and Freudo–Marxian paradigms, we have seen dogmas of beliefs and notions of reason. As the author unfolds, Aryans have walked through the evolutionary struggles through the ambiguous peaks and valleys with triumph and defeat in the world's two most ancient religions: Vedic and Zoroastrian. They both left behind stories of war between gods and demons. Perhaps private property, as Rousseau held, emerged subsequently and the owners of pieces of land became rivals.

Expressions and practices of Vedic libido are reflected in ancient hymns and temples that demonstrate the art, aesthetics of what may be called obscene in pseudo-modern world.[20] Khajuraho, the Sun Temple and Vātsyāyana's *Kama Sutra* are evidence-based manifestations of mystified sex.

---

[19] Saraswati: While ONGC will soon start drilling in six different locations in the state of Haryana, India, Archaeological Survey of India (ASI) has collected samples of the water from Mugalwali village. http://economictimes.indiatimes.com/news/politics-and-nation/haryana-sweet-water-pools-fire-up-saraswati-revival/articleshow/47229565.cms (accessed on 4 December 2017).

[20] https://truthabouthinduism.wordpress.com/2014/05/15/there-is-indeed-obscenity-in-vedas/ (accessed on 24 May 2015).

It is widely believed that George Lucas's *Star Wars* classic is abstractly based on the Hindu philosophy. It is a galactic saga cinematically manifested through the perpetual struggle between virtues and evil, similar to the struggle between Devas (gods) and Asuras (demons), throughout the Aryan history. Hitler gave a bad name to the Aryan values by using Swastika as a symbol of racial superiority that culminated into the Holocaust. Many fundamentalist scholars continue to use this pernicious view to perpetuate their nefarious interests. Much of contemporary world's continued violence, bigotry and terror are driven by those evil belief systems, which have no room in civil discourse.

The trajectory of human evolution is embedded in perpetual greed, gloom and gore, which are rationalized by ideological predilections and territorial trappings driven by the lust for hegemonic power. Watch HBO's *Game of Thrones*. It is all about mayhem, sex and slavery. Aryans were not angels. They were humans. Demonization and deification, as Devas and Asuras of the Vedas practised in their arctic wisdom. May be Rousseau was close to truth: It is the rise of property that eventually led to the emergence of civility at the expense of innate human innocence. Genesis is a story of human evolution and devolution at the same time. I have argued elsewhere that Buddha and his teachings represented a protest against the Vedic decadence manifested by ritualistic violence and unmitigated human sufferings. Since there is neither any God, nor any war in Buddhism, it is reasonable to believe that the Vedic establishment of Varanasi was threatened by Buddha's discourses. He had to move to Sarnath to offer his wisdom. There is evidence to connect Buddhist impact on Nietzschean dictum, 'God is dead'.

We are on the cusp of a new era of ambiguous hope: *Faith* and *reason* are entangled in a mongoose and cobra fight. ISIS threatens the State, the very foundation of a civil society.

The burden of this introductory chapter is to underscore the fact that the world's two greatest democracies—the United States and India—are emblematic of the new and old orthodoxies of power that still subjugate marginalized people. It is a daunting challenge to any messiah of equality to fundamentally transform the order.

Just the way caste and 'casteism' persist in India, slavery and its remains haunt Americans. Confederate monuments in southern states remind us of a shameful past. The need to remove them represent an American Dilemma.

'A group of psychiatrists has written to Congress warning that Donald Trump poses a "clear and present danger" to the world'.[21] The spectre of Trumpian neopragmatism is alarming. Its impact on public policy and social services is going to be regressive for many years. As violence, terror and insecurity rise, politico–cultural suppression will manifest in deadly forms and shapes.

In *the other* world, cow vigilantes terrorize Muslims in India.[22] India's civil society, in many ways, is like post-American culture. *Unfreedom* and populist leaders thrive on people's ignorance and superstitious beliefs. A rapist Guru's conviction is protested by his followers leaving many people dead. He defined his sect as 'a non-profit social welfare and spiritual organization'.[23] Social welfare as an institution is prostituted by charlatans in a hyper-democracy. The great challenge of the twenty-first century is not to restore social welfare; it is basically elimination of the need for it.

Sciences in general and social sciences in particular should assume some responsibility for their malevolent uses and abuses. In 2008 the market crashed and *economists* failed to predict, let alone prevent. Why waste a precious Nobel and its intrinsic validation power on inane

---

[21] https://www.yahoo.com/news/psychiatrists-tell-congress-donald-trump-074136725.html (accessed on 4 December 2017).

[22] http://www.npr.org/sections/parallels/2017/05/02/526426203/vigilantes-in-india-protecting-sacred-cows-promoting-a-hindu-way-of-life (accessed on 14 August 2017).

[23] 'The flamboyant chief of the Dera Sacha Sauda sect, Gurmeet Ram Rahim Singh, has been convicted of rape by an Indian court. The sect claims to have more than 60 million followers around the world and the 50-year-old "godman" is revered by his supporters. But, he is no stranger to controversy. In 2002, Mr Singh was investigated by India's federal police for murder and alleged rape, charges he has denied. He has also been accused of forcing 400 of his followers to undergo castration so they could "get closer to god"'. http://www.bbc.com/news/world-asia-india-41047531 (accessed on 25 August 2017).

intellectuals? To paraphrase Paulo Coelho, we ought to 'help bring out the *Warrior of Light* within each of us' (1998: 173).

> That's the Philosopher's stone and the Elixir of Life. It's Master Work of the alchemists. Whoever swallows the elixir will never be sick again, and a fragment from the stone turns any metal into gold. (Coelho 1998: 138)

CHAPTER 2

The World of Welfare

*What is happening is the discovery (or rather, rediscovery) of
nature as an ally in the struggle against the exploitative societies
in which the violation of nature aggravates the violation of man.
The discovery of the liberating forces of nature and their vital
role in the construction of a free society becomes a new force
of social change.*

—Herbert Marcuse (1972: 59).

Thomas D. Watts, an eminent professor of SW, introduced his book
with the first chapter entitled 'Introducing the "World" of Social
Welfare' (1990). His 'world' 27 years ago marked the beginning of
an end. Social welfare, as he and his co-editors designed, represented
different countries where social policies and social services embodied
social programmes to cater to certain human needs which people
could not fulfil themselves. Ever since, the Welfare State has been in
disarray. Public mistrust in the so-called 'entitlements' and the rise
of both individualism and conservative ideologies transformed the
American creed. As Eveline E. Burns, the mother of social policy,
would say, 'America has become mean'.[1]

---

[1] Personal conversation after Ronald Reagan became the President.

Welfare, Policy and Social Work

As I assumed the office of Dean, School of Social Welfare at Louisiana State University in 1981, I was advised by a host of distinguished alumni to change the school's name. My own professional commitment to advance SW education per se also reinforced the change. 'Welfare' was replaced by 'work'. The relationship between 'work' and 'welfare' has never been more intriguing than now.

Welfare, as I see, is a benign field, like health and education. By that logic, if 'health' involves 'ill-health', 'welfare' cannot be separated from 'ill-fare'. The New Deal followed by the Great Society and its massive 'war against poverty' changed America forever. The civil rights movement pumped the oxygen that policymakers needed so badly.

If people did not have 'work', unemployment compensation came handy. If people lacked adequate income and fell below the poverty line, society offered them public assistance, including housing. Poor and indigent people did not have to depend on the residual safety net during illness, deformity and old age. Medicaid and Medicare with other related programmes basically institutionalized social needs and the means to cover cradle to grave exigencies of life.

SW's professional roles could not be exaggerated in this process. From establishing eligibility to providing counselling and advocacy, social workers stood ready to 'help' the *clients*. What does this nexus involve? To elaborate this process, it is perhaps crucial to define the parameters of the concepts involved in the 'world of social welfare'. Lest, we may lose the desired focus, I shall confine my attempt to clarify the basic working components and constructs of this domain which mainly includes:

- Social welfare
- Social work
- Social policy
- Social action and community organization
- Social research
- Social development

There is a gamut of roles and tasks associated with each professional activity that we include in SW. The interrelatedness and implicit overlaps in these realms of intervention is usually field-specific targeting a particular population with socialized methodologies of 'help'.

Authors from Thomas D. Watts to Walter Friedlander (1975) offered a great community service to define these concepts and methods, and textbooks are awash with chapters without new wheels invented. When I discuss SW, I am not ignorant of its traditional methods and fields. Casework, group work, community organization, social action and research continue to be part of generalized, advanced practice models liberally defined by various schools as it suits their needs and accreditation requirements. There are, however, a few notions and formulations that I would like to discuss in this context. Thomas Watts' prescience is on the point:

> As our world grows smaller, our vision and our worldview about social welfare must increase. We can take steps toward becoming 'citizens of the world' instead of merely citizens of our home country or region (1990: 9)

Long before Paul Diesing (1982) wrote *Science & Ideology in the Policy Sciences*, I signified policy sciences as a major force for analysis and action that may help actualize social transformation.

World Citizenry

Techno–digital advancements and globalized economy with rise of inequality in the industrialized world has created a new world of connected dissonance which implies attached detachment. Brexit is an example. China's new Silk Road is another neo-expansionist project. American nativism and India's nationalism are not much different. In such a self-interest-focused world any conversation about 'world citizenry' sounds unrealistic, put politely. My belated sense of reality is: Equality is an ideal; it is like world peace. The Middle-East meltdown of stately order and spread of radicalized Islam has destroyed even the myth of global peace and justice. In such a poisoned social climate, social work and social welfare have a definite role but the required tools of intervention are muffled with regressive public and social policies that do not allow, let alone help, any regional and global involvement with needed resources.

Refugees in and outside Syria, Iraq and Afghanistan present an international crisis beyond any SW programme. Anti-immigration laws in the United States and the wave of 'we' and 'they' slogans is beyond rational professional intervention.

1. A SW instructor just launched a blog: Socialworkersuccess.com.[2] 'In today's post, I'm going to share nine life lessons social workers can learn from how Prince styled his life,' said Lolita Boykin—using Nate Crowell's words—after legendry musician Prince's death. Create your own path.
2. Develop more than one skill.
3. Advocate for yourself.
4. Share some of your best stuff.
5. Find your confidence.
6. Stay connected.
7. Embrace diversity.
8. Find your 'thing'.
9. Create a will.

'Whether you are a fan of Prince's music or not, you have to respect his creativity, boldness and authenticity. His life and music clearly impacted many people, myself included'. A few weeks later, the same learned professor posts 'Social Work for Profit' on LinkedIn.

Boykin's lessons of success—the emerging trend—are couched in the language of grief and greed; they relate to American SW's heart with little impact to transform the world beyond their private practice.[3]

---

[2] http://socialworkersuccess.com/prince-life-lessons/ (accessed on 12 August 2017).

[3] One glaring example is an expertly authored new book by Neil Gilbert (2017) *Never Enough: Capitalism and the Progressive Spirit* (2017). Gilbert, a reputed Berkeley scholar, chants the mantras of free market economy that has brought 'progressive conservatism'. It is akin to George W. Bush' 'compassionate

A comparative perspective, I believe, is helpful to assess the human condition in relation to a particular practice and discipline.

Comparative Human–Social Development: A Policy Perspective

Social work and its related components within the orbit of social welfare include a new sphere which may be named 'human–social (comparative) development' (HSCD). It is not yet a recognized specialty by any of our professional organizations and their leaders. Their limited vocabularies do include SD which is a dated and fallacious concept. HSCSD's policy perspective trumps the traditional model of social work practice (SWP) as Figure 2.1 seeks to demonstrate.

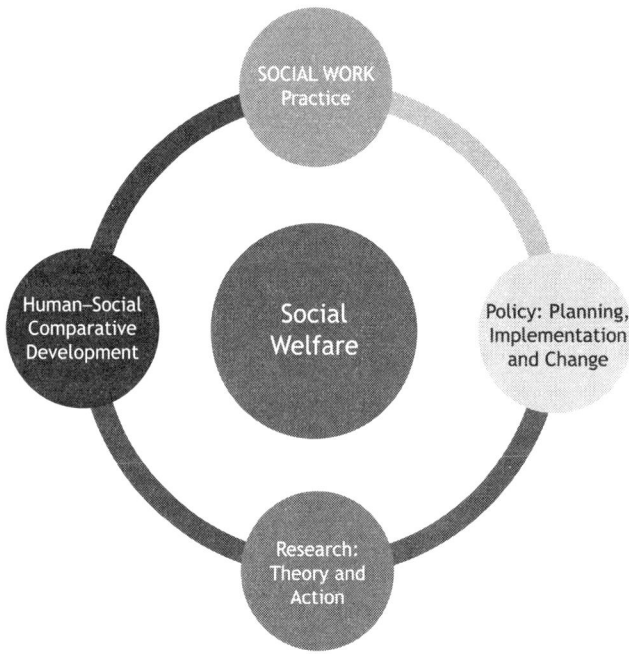

Figure 2.1 *The World of 'Social Welfare'*

---

conservatism' which destroyed Iraq on false premises. SW educators and practitioners usually follow this model of 'transformation' and 'development'.

Whenever social workers in the United States feel disappointed in their profession, they talk about social development as a new apostle of hope. They begin with Amartya Sen's quote, invite a few marketable lords and end up with a symposium or two with no consequence, except networking for continued personal promotion. Ideological and institutional promotions lend validity to this wildly successful model of leadership.

Social development is an entry in the *Encyclopedia of Social Work*. Entries in the *Encyclopedia* are invited and selected by an editorial board of presumed expertise. I contributed 'International Social Welfare: Comparative Systems' (1987: 957–969) to its 18th volume. Now, *Comparative Social Welfare* is excluded despite an invited submission by this author.[4]

My three immediately preceding books (2007, 2011, 2015) have made an argument for a new perspective on social development per se. I see social and human developments as two symbiotic sides of the same coin. Also, I postulate that (a) social–human development, as a process, cannot be fully understood without (b) comparative analysis and methodology. Therefore, it is HSCSD that is required for all SW graduates. This formulation is premised on the *unification of social work* education and practice (Mohan 1999). These important and related concepts relevant to this discussion are defined further:

Comparative social welfare

> seeks to analyze the relative impact on, and interdependence of, existing social orders that tend to determine the nature and scope of social services in different countries. Implied here is an assumption that a particular social welfare system interacts with, and is influenced by, other systems and a comparative approach is a possible vehicle for mutual understanding and assessment toward better cross-cultural relations. (Mohan 1985a: 2)

Social welfare literature usually tends to use 'international social work/ welfare' as 'comparative social welfare', often interchangeably so.

---

[4] Arbitrary inclusion and exclusion designs manufactured knowledge which defeats its purpose.

This is a conceptual–methodological error. Richard J. Estes (1984) and Christian Aspalter (2006) are the only two other theorists who have made a clearer distinction between the two related but different concepts. Comparative social welfare's significance cannot be overstated in an increasingly complex world. 'The study of similarities and differences forms logical basis for the classification, analysis, and conceptual synthesis of differential systems' (Mohan 1987: 957).

HSCSD is not an amalgamation of varied sub-disciplines; it is a synthetic unification of integrated whole that incubates and nurtures the entire process of personality development in a complex environment. I would argue that HSCSD replaced *human behaviour and social environment* (HBSE) as a required sequence in SW curriculum.

Of special significance is the status and role of social policy in the vocabularies of welfare and work. Fortunately, social policy is the most fertile field. Unfortunately, it also is the most lucrative area where required expensive texts fill the market. Obviously, there is no perfect and complete definition of social (welfare) policy since points of emphases differ from author to author. My take on the subject remains unchanged. I view social policy as a codeterminant of economic policy. It is difficult to see it as an independent variable in the variegated process of social and economic needs and policies. As such:

> Social policy is a creative decision-making process that involves a complex system of cognitive offshoots and politico–socio–economic variables undergirding a unified whole of transcendental values and techno–scientific advancements. Policymaking is a tough value-oriented balancing of probabilities rather than hunt for convenient possibilities. Yet, policy quintessentially is a science and art of the possible. Social policy ought to be conceptualized as a possible theory and practice of the preferred societal values, goals and interventions. The range of social policy includes: alternatives that economize resources and optimize human function without oppression, values that humanize services and programs without degradation, allocations that generate creative mechanisms without ugly political maneuvers, and strategies that promote conducive social arrangements without counterproductive results. (Mohan 1985: 5–6)

The definition just offered may be noted for its universality and prescience. One may examine the post-Obama debates and politics of the Trump administration whose signature policy issue continues to repeal and change Obama Care, that is, Affordable Health Care Act.[5] The same standard could also be applied to Trump's immigration and foreign policy demonstrating how porous and political policymaking process is.

Social Action, Community Organization and Research

SW research wallows in its nascence. While meaningful public policy and practice researches are conducted by cognate discipline, social workers researchers contend with issues, clients, pedagogy, surveys and exploratory research designs that help graduates earn doctorates with much impact on communities. Elsewhere, I contend elimination of both undergraduate and doctoral levels with greater emphasis on the quality of graduate degrees (Masters in Social Work, MSW). Doctor of Medicine (MD) and Juris Doctor (JD) are terminal degrees in medicine and law. If knowledge and truth cannot be the outcomes of research, mere benefits of funded grants cannot substitute for culture of science. SW's illiberal liberalism and partisan groups do not help achieve relative legitimacy. 'Science is one of the things that people do, and therefore it can be studied in the same way that other human activities are studied' (Diesing 1982: 1).

---

[5] 'The **Affordable Health Care for America Act** (or **HR 3962** was a bill that was crafted by the United States House of Representatives in October 29th of 2009. It never became law as originally drafted. At the encouragement of the Obama administration, the 111th Congress devoted much of its time to enacting reform of the United States' health care system. Known as the "House bill," HR 3962 was the House of Representatives' chief legislative proposal during the health reform debate. On December 24, 2009, the Senate passed an alternative health care bill, the Patient Protection and Affordable Care Act (H.R. 3590). In 2010, the House abandoned its reform bill in favor of amending the Senate bill (via the reconciliation process) in the form of the Health Care and Education Reconciliation Act of 2010'. https://en.wikipedia.org/wiki/Affordable_Health_Care_for_America_Act (accessed on 12 August 2017).

Our contemporary social science research in general—and SW research in particular—is fraught with perceived alternate reality unrelated to the roots of causes. What Ravets (1971) called 'shoddy science' and 'industrialization of research' (cited by Diesing 1982: 247) is a befitting characterisation. To quote Paul Diesing, 'it appears that the dynamics of a professionalised social science include ever-increasing specialization, division of labor in research, ever-expanding research budgets, geometrically expanding publication rates, and ever more rapid obsolescence of research' (1982: 247). The continued factional emphasis in this area is confounding.[6] The so-called research centres in major schools and departments of SW basically involve grantsmanship; multi-authored journal articles justify and procure funds and promote principal grant writer. Research becomes a means to material ends rather than a vehicle of knowledge. Picketty has a point:

> It is illusionary, I believe, to think that scholar and the citizen live in separate moral universes, the former concerned with means and the latter with ends. Although comprehensive, this view ultimately strikes me as dangerous. (2014: 574)

---

[6] Manohar Pawar has to be congratulated for launching *Community and Social Development Journal* (SAGE 2017). The issue is: How and why 'community' and 'social development' are the only two connections in these widely important fields? Is 'community' the only crucial component in 'social development'? Or, does the latter deal with 'community' only? Sometimes intellectual coherence is sacrificed for practical reasons at the expense of theoretical congruence and integrity. Two academic silos do not make a good discipline.

CHAPTER 3

Plateaus and Platitudes of Practice

'He is a prodigy', he said at last, 'he is an emissary of pity, and science, and progress, and devil knows what else. We want', he began to declaim suddenly, 'for the guidance of the cause entrusted to us by Europe, so to speak, higher intelligence, wide sympathies, a singleness of purpose'.
—Joseph Conrad, *Heart of Darkness* (1995: 53).

Plateaus and platitudes of practice (PPP) represent the ambiguities of hope amidst unfathomable human miseries. The banality of suffering and sickness has evoked strong feelings in the hearts of people. Siddhartha became the Buddha. I became a lecturer in SW (1964). The emergence of altruistic responses, individual and institutional, represents a benign trajectory of helping others. The *others* in this context have been the victims of misfortunes, human ingenuity or perhaps both. Perhaps nature's wrath—to some extent—is also a consequence of human arrogance. Ignorance is the womb of knowledge.

Plateaus of Thought

In his Foreword to Gilles Deleuze and Félix Guattari's *A Thousand Plateaus: Capitalism and Schizophrenia*, Brian Massumi comments about official philosophy that breeds the 'discourse of sovereign judgement, of stable subjectivity legislated by "good" sense of rocket like identity, universal truth, and (white male) justice' ([1987] 2011: ix).

Examination of contemporary SW's ontology and ethos is in order. The attempt here is to offer a clearer vision of both human conditions and societal arrangements that seek to mitigate metastasizing forces of oppression.

Professionalization of 'help' and 'altruism' is the hallmark of modern SW. Modernity, however, is fraught with pretention and mendacity. SW has become a slogan and shibboleth. The very exclusivity of knowledge that it claimed for its professional status is lost in the fog of welfare confusion, complexity of human nature and conundrums of public debates. SW as the world knows today is a by-product of Judeo–Christian morality and ethics which enshrined the post-War Welfare State ideology. Massumi minces no words:

> 'State philosophy' is another word for the representational thinking that has characterized Western metaphysics since Plato, but has suffered an at least momentary setback during the last quarter century at the hands of Jacques Derrida, Michel Foucault, and poststructuralist theory generally. As described by Deleuze, it reposes on a double identity: of the thinking subject, and of the subjects it creates and to which it lends its own presumed attributes of sameness and consistency. (2011: xi)

The basic premise of state welfare is to maintain status quo without unbearable pain and stress. Professionalizing social services means containment, entitlement and institutionalized help. Again, Massumi sums up:

> The subject, its concepts, and also the objects in the world to which the concepts are applied have a shared, internal essence: the self-resemblance at the basis of identity. Representational thought is analogical; its concern is to establish correspondence between symmetrically structured domains. The faculty of judgment is the policeman of analogy, assuring that each of the three terms

is honestly itself, and that the proper correspondences obtain. In thought its end is truth, in action justice. (2011: xi)

The rational foundation of order insures state employment of professionals and philosophers. More recently, private sector, NGOs and individual–group practitioners have also become more visible. But the State has its hegemonic power. Issuance of licenses, distribution and allocation of funded grants, regulation of public education, policies and their implementation according to legal statutes are principal determinants of principles of truth: equality, diversity and social justice.

By the laws of serendipity, however, contradictions and counter-productivity surface reality. This alternate reality, I believe, is the focus and justification of contemporary SWP. To validate this observation, I subject a few flagship publications at national and international level. First, *Social Work: A Journal of the National Association of Social Workers* July 2017, 62, 3: 193–288. A few observations are offered further as a critique of the contents.

The editorial reduces much of SW to 'families in practice' which offers opportunities 'to advance scientific knowledge and practice strategies of the field' (p. 198). Can we really achieve scientific knowledge about subjective realities at a juncture when social institutions, by and large, are melting down?

Most of the articles in the volume, by design, are focused on violence, 'reproductive justice', 'sexuality within social work' discourse, group work and resilience, curriculum for native American adolescents, social security and 'conservation in social sciences'. While none of these topics is beyond SW, none of the pieces demonstrates the depth of analytical skills. Statistical tables are poor substitutes for sociological imagination. The 'positive discourse on sexuality' hardly incorporates a reference, let alone sociological imagination, to Foucault's classic three volumes on human sexuality (227–234). A doctoral student's commentary on 'conservation social sciences' is full of naïveté and wish-fulfilment without a critical understanding of the nature and ethos of social sciences (275–278). Her conclusion—'Conservation was ready for social work'—is both hasty and self-serving.

A closer examination of the articles contained in this flagship volume reveals inclusion of Hijab and depression as well as Christian faith and SW. While new issues are welcome, a revisionist emphasis on faith (and spirituality) seems unsettling.

The other journal is *International Social Work*. Its 60th anniversary issue just appeared online.[1] International social welfare organizations network resources that somewhat mitigate human misery without touching the basic root causes.[2] If 'HIV is a disease with its roots in inequality',[3] scourges must be annihilated at the roots which implies more than treatment and alliterated symposia. Other articles covering different countries mainly address issues related to refugees, asylum seekers, immigration, diaspora, sex trafficking, partner violence, disability and discrimination. Miseries that date back to antiquity cannot be wiped out without changing the calculus of life as lived by helpless people.

Journal of Social Work Education published by the Council on Social Work Education (CSWE) continues to recycle vocational pedagogy without much enlightenment for a creative and critical mind. A perusal of these flagship publications also indicates some troubling findings:

---

[1] http://journals.sagepub.com/toc/iswb/60/3?utm_source=Adestra&utm_medium=email&utm_content=Read%20the%20anniversary%20issue&utm_campaign=7J0030&utm_term= (accessed on 7 July 2017).

[2] IFSW Europe: International Federation of Social Workers hold today its first day of the Global Executives Meeting. IFSW Europe is represented by President Ana Isabel Lima Fernandez and Vice-president Ana Radulescu. Regional reports were presented with really positives outcomes: The Federation has grown 40 per cent in the last years; the executive structures in all regions are consolidated; celebrations of social work development (SWD) in all regions is a reality; there have been regional conferences in Puerto Rico, China, Iceland and Tanzania and policies and statements have been developed in all regions. IFSW Global works together with the IFSW regions to strengthen the SW profession and the role of SW practitioners in different professionals fields: politics, economics, climatic change, sustainability, social services and so on. https://www.facebook.com/ifsw.europe?hc_ref=NEWSFEED (accessed on 9 July 2017).

[3] Tom Finn, Director of the Coordinating Comprehensive Care for Children (4Children), shared his views at the 4th Annual Global Service Workforce Alliance Symposium, Washington, DC [*NASW News* 62, no. 7 (July 2017): 1].

Rise of collaborative–joint–guest authorship, a nearly incestuous review process and referencing and an apparently predatory mentorship that employs students' work as a group endeavour—is a rampant behavior amongst social work scholars. The fact is evident by near extinction of independent, solo authorship which is a sad development. The academic neurosis of promotion and tenure has further encouraged anti-intellectual, sometimes unfair and unworthy, practices that perpetuate a beguiled culture of parasitic mediocrity. Commercially and organizationally published expensive 'required texts' simply perpetuate the kitsch. The *Encyclopedia of Social Work* published every 10 years or so is a showcase of relevant and irrelevant subjects in various fields as selected, commissioned and approved by a group of editors. The whole process of publishing manufactured knowledge as state-of-the-art volumes, as I experienced and saw, looked both arbitrary and less than intellectual.

Social Practice: Social Work's False Consciousness

Understanding of 'social reality' must be a prerequisite to any social (work) intervention. Most American SW students and faculty, however, lack any knowledge of 'social construction of reality' (Berger and Luckmann 1967). Social thought is alien to these careerists masquerading as rebels. The question is: What is their cause?

A society that puts premium on social status, roles and class is inherently inimical to achieving equality and justice. As such, a 'false consciousness' serves as a tool to achieving righteous goals and objectives. The rise and fall of the Welfare State/society may be seen in light of this reality. No wonder why the chasm between *society* and *State* has never been that deeper. President Donald Trump has the lowest ratings; yet his 'societal' support remains unchanged. This baffling paradox is product of 'false consciousness'. Much of public and social policy is an outcome of this mindset that resorts to incrementalism and minimalism in the game of governance.

Nineteenth-century German thought is mainly attributed to three stems of thought—'the Marxian, the Nietzschean, and the historicist'— (Berger and Luckmann 1967: 7)—which fundamentally changed the conceptual lens to study humans in society. No SW curriculum at any level is designed to incorporate post-War Franco-German continental thought that shifted the paradigm relative to human–social reality.

Race matters; so, does class, perhaps more than race. Plateaus of perspectives so widely vary that truth has escaped close analysis. The myth of a classless society does not discourage discussion on equality, a notion that persists in a painfully unequal world. Pundits invented 'social justice' as a unifying indicator for unwarranted inequality and injustice long before the Enlightenment. The age of reason has fuelled the engines of anger. The complexity of social issues is challenging. Crime is on decline but violence and terror are not. Likewise, wealth has increased but inequality is on the rise.

This book is about social practice. The structure of SP differs from variants of traditional and modern SW. SW at this stage of its evolution, I contend, is a model based on dated ideologies and incongruent concepts confounding its legitimacy and effectiveness. *Social practice as conceptualized here is a discursive idea of transformative practice that might lead to a post-human condition.*

The premised postulates of this kind of 'practice' is not the reinvention of a wheel. It is a reflective critique of what is more appropriate and congruent with human reality. SW, putatively an altruistic endeavour, still seeks the status of a profession. Will this organized enterprise help resolve human–social problems that we confront today?

In a digitally regulated world, I believe, the meanings of both *social* and *work* have changed. This calls for innovative thinking on the cusp of the 'fourth' revolution. *The goal of social work should be the end of itself.*

Modelled after North American experiences, varied indigenized forms—and bases of practice—have evolved over the last hundred years or so. True, modern SW is an American invention. But world realities have changed. Emulation of foreign models to fix local and regional problems is only justified if the remedy were a pair of blue jeans. Curricular designs, modalities of teaching and patterns of practical training cannot be replicated in a diverse and complex world. Strength, evidence, competency and other bases of professional practice still lack authenticity and professional credence. The universality of values and culturally specific issues are not always congruent. To mix the two is problematic.

Times have changed since the emergence of SW as a quasi-professional enterprise. Post-War conditions brought the era of welfare which shaped the structure and rationale of social services. 9/11 heralded political terror, cyber insecurity and ubiquitous fear. Despite globalization, inequality amongst nations widened. Digital revolution, the Arab Spring and certain anti-State movements promoted chaotic populist revolts that shattered the old dynamic of inter- and intrasocietal relationships.

Silicon Valley start-ups, models, values, lifestyles and corresponding personal and social issues create illusions of hope. Uberization of services and information revolution have, ironically, triggered Darwinian outcomes. The nature of work has changed. Soon, work may not exist. The end of work is the beginning of a new culture where SW per se will have become totally irrelevant. I believe we are already there; it is only organizational displacement and dissonance that keep the phantom alive.

Jonathan Taplin in his unsettling book *Move Fast and Break Things* (2017) alerts how Facebook, Google and Amazon media companies have destroyed democracy.[4] Social media has unleashed unstoppable forces of change. 'A stinging polemic that traces the destructive monopolization of the Internet by Google, Facebook and Amazon, and that proposes a new future for musicians, journalists, authors and filmmakers in the digital age'.[5] Other professions, mainly social in nature, may not even survive.

---

[4] As a precursor to this book, the reader may find this piece from *London Review of Books* rather interesting. https://www.lrb.co.uk/v39/n16/john-lanchester/you-are-the-product?utm_campaign=Revue%20newsletter&utm_medium=Newsletter&utm_source=Om%20Malik (accessed on 4 December 2017).

[5] https://www.amazon.com/Move-Fast-Break-Things-Undermined/dp/0316275778/ref=la_B01N374FXT_1_1?s=books&ie=UTF8&qid=1506278607&sr=1-1 (accessed on 24 September 2017).

Work as invented by our civilization will morph into apps. 'Social' as a qualifying prefix will become redundant as social institutions continue to melt down. Simple algorithms will wipe out all the tasks, skills and checklists that therapists and social service workers employ with protective 'licenses'. No one likes an unlicensed neurosurgeon; however, licensing as a means to exclude dissent amounts to censorship.

SW, as I proclaimed two decades ago, ought to be an end of itself. Using it as a means to career paths does make a pragmatic sense but its ethos is lost when systemic aetiologies of suffering deepen. No problem has ever been solved without uprooting its causes. Social work's cardinal sin has been to ignore this basic fact. Notions of 'help', 'care', 'healing' have reinforced dubious—often misleading and counterproductive—traditional practices of altruism and therapy that perpetuate the myth of poverty as a cultural issue. (Mohan 2011; 2015). Much of social science research and policy formulation has been an outcome of this pernicious mythology.

SW's pivotal mission centres around social justice as a concept. In reality, there is nothing that professionally 'licensed' social workers do to achieve social justice. This moral dissonance is perhaps the main reason of its inanity and irrelevance. Doctors cure patients; engineers build bridges; lawyers defend and prosecute. What do social workers exactly do? Help others? Reform society? Solve personal social problems? Formulate social policy? The leaders who perform these noble acts are seldom professional social workers. Professionals simply deal with alternate reality.

SW as a profession will cease to exist as apps, robotics and algorithms take on human specializations. Autonomous self-driven cars, online education, robotic surgery, online medicine and incredible feats of artificial intelligence bluntly replace flawed human capacities. Lordy, computers still do not hallucinate!

Intellectually spayed, SW is sustained by the lingering edifice of the 'social Welfare State' and its allies. 'Welfare' has become a dirty word. Welfare backlash, political convenience, bureaucratic corruption, myopic public policies and a new class and caste war have practically abandoned the victims of a 'rigged system'. Briefly stated, social transformation of human needs, institutional deconstruction and new economic–political linkages are required to synergize the system. Failure of social and political sciences accounts for ineffectual, often misleading, scenarios of hope.

Fault Lines: Globalization and Class War

Wilhelm von Humboldt's goal—"spiritual and moral training of the nation"—unified three ideals: truth, justice, and the State which forged a moral relationship between philosophy and the government. This phallogocentric model of thought is opposed to 'nomad thought' which is akin to Nietzschean 'gay science'. *Nomos is* an open-ended space rather than *logos*, the citadel of power (Massumi 2011: xii–xiii). This well-intended but misconstrued focus is what Thomas Szasz called 'liberation by oppression' (2004).

The 'client–practitioner' dyad is a perfect embodiment of this stately ordained system. SW ethics, practice, education, training and research are fundamentally hierarchized duality of power to justify the needs of the state which seeks humanization in a therapeutic society. Any crime or horror committed by the villains of civility instantly becomes a 'mental health' issue. Addiction and substance abuse treatment programmes are generously funded. Military SW becomes a sexy specialization. Regulation of 'deviance' as varied behavioural therapies is the basis of academic exclusions, which spiritualizes the Ivory Tower.

Class war did not end with fall of the Berlin Wall. It has been there in some form ever since poverty was invented at the end of primitive innocence. Modern civility rests on the tombstone of primitive innocence.

The new revolt of the masses, both in India and the United States, has lately brought two populist leaders who use democracy to reinforce authoritarianism with exclusionary trappings. The ideal of an inclusive civil society is eclipsed by the forces of reaction and unreason (Mohan 2017).[6]

---

[6] https://www.academia.edu/29372061/White_Trash_and_the_Deplorables_Continued_Crisis_of_Men_in_America (accessed on 5 December 2017).

Tribal–cyber forces will determine the future mechanisms and models of SP. The interdependence and multilinearity of this complex nexus will define the nature of new professions and academic endeavours. The future of SW depends on the coming nature of 'work'. The inevitable changes, I contend, will be affected by a pervasive climate of techno-terror and artificial intelligence that will transform society into a dystopian *leviathan*.

Michel Foucault's theory of 'governmentality' inspired me to formulate two related concepts: *departmentality* and *developmentality*. Much of higher education in America and elsewhere is in throes of this two-faceted crisis. Academic territoriality, institutional–individual narcissism and corrupted standards of excellence arbitrarily applied in the name of diversity and ethnic notions breed academic parasitism and mediocrity which thwart the development of social consciousness amongst younger generations. Developmentalists delude themselves when they talk of 'social development' without comprehending its flawed assumptions.

We are guilty of bad faith, knowingly offering something that we ourselves do not commit to—and by proselytizing—amounts to malpractice. The flat-earthers of SW education still fail to comprehend the nature of twenty-first century's challenges. Self-indulgent arrogance of the professional elites in the Ivory Tower is anti-intellectual and counterproductive. Academia is increasingly sceptical of SW's authenticity as a discipline. No wonder why schools of SW are being widely demoted to departmental units under the umbrella of less than respected disciplines. Ignorance is the fount of knowledge. Arrogance leads to hubris.

Emerging human–robot relationships will replace and shape much of what social workers do as practitioners. My main concern is about the integrity and legitimacy of our profession, which is a prerequisite to social transformation. Infused across the entire interdisciplinary spectrum, rather than departmentally hierarchized with minimalist approaches, SP may yield some result. Humans will remain human. Personal and social problems shall continue so long as mortals remain victims of their own trappings. SW lacks, what Foucault calls, 'the will to know'.

Constructs of knowledge, skills, methods, techniques and values of *social practice* may have a greater level of effectiveness and authenticity that we painfully lack in contemporary *social [work] practice*. Much of this volume offers aspects of this sense of self-awareness whose subjective–objective reality will depend on the reader's vantage point. In closing, real and hypothetical formulations presented in this book seek to validate my main thesis: Humans evolve; developmentality will devolve compassion into a vocation and departmentality will degrade disciplinarities under the cover of science. Techno-hubris will shape human needs and services as functionally designed by its own necessities.

Internationalization of social work (ISW) in a globalized world is a natural outcome. However, social realties and politico–cultural differences in a hopelessly divided world dictate common-sense applications and adaptations to professional practices that seek progressive social changes. Paradoxical time requires multilinearity of pathways.

Global SW, like world peace, is more of a slogan than reality.[7] Likewise, ISW is more of a field of interest than a discipline. However, possibilities of growing this specialty abound if 'specialists' focus more on issues rather than resumes.

---

[7] I gave a presentation on social work without borders at CSWE, APM 2007/2008. I reached nowhere for lack of network–institutional support.

CHAPTER 4

Archaeology of Social Practice

Happiness, in the reduced sense in which we recognize it as possible, is a problem of the economics of the individual's libido. There is no golden rule which applies to every one: every man must find out for himself in what particular fashion he can be saved.
—Sigmund Freud (1961: 30).

The Will for Well-being

In his brilliant discourse *The Archaeology of Knowledge*, Foucault says:

> There was a time when archaeology, as a discipline devoted to silent monuments, inert traces, objects without context, and things left by the past, aspired to the condition of history, and attained meaning only through the reinstitution of a historical discourse; it might be said, to play on words a little, that in our time history aspires to the condition of archaeology, to the intrinsic description of the monument. (1972: 7)

Social practice is human carpentry of fractured relationships and institutions that adversely affect the human condition. Archaeologically, it is a search for monumental constructs that civilization is built upon. People, property and pugnacity constructed a civil order that eventually civilized the barbarians. This was the first social transformation of human society.

Archaeology, in Foucauldian terms, is deeper understanding of historical phenomenon. The basic premise of this book is to unravel *social practice* as a ritual of reform employed by humans in self-preservation with or without consciousness of transformative impact.

We live in post-Dickensian times punctuated by fear and freedom. Terrorism in the age of digital revolution is a baffling social phenomenon that defies explanation and resolution. X goes to Iraq; returns with a wounded soul (post-traumatic stress disorder, PTSD?) and goes berserk as a mass murderer in school, club, airport and anywhere. Mental health issues play proxy to validate a horrific tragedy. This counter-truth, I contend, has become the basis of a therapeutic society that shields unreason against any meaningful 'social practice'. Societal failure to annihilate the genesis of unmitigated misery is a reason to double down therapeutic and rehabilitative services.

SW as profession grew out of the burdens of poverty, modernity and war. War against poverty brought the Great Society, which is now faltering, in the post-ideological fog. War against war continues abated in different theatres with new geopolitical dynamics. The reality is: We remain a failed civilization, hopelessly mired in the hubris of the Age of Reason.

'American Carnage'[1] may be an exaggerated description of an unhinged social panoramic profile: broken souls, shattered lives, dystopic communities. And a dead 'social contract'. In the postulated context, we examine how relevant, appropriate and valid is it to perpetuate the practices that are neither effective nor relevant in the corporatized, global, 'administrative states'. A requiem for the welfarism is in order.

The core of American social welfare policy is populist, and as William Epstein argues, 'romantic'. He has a point: 'The immense growth in American wealth and thus its capacity to address material

---

[1] An exaggerated epitaph labelled by President Donald Trump.

deprivation has not translated into political will to address the nation's social problems' (2017: xiii).

Welfare State, Crisis and Legitimacy

We live in a divided, troubled world. The fundamental ethical pillars of all SPs—confidentiality, self-determination, face-to-face communication—are myths that practitioners thrive on. It is not the reality that is bothersome; it is the artful concealment of the facts— alternative reality—that constitutes malpractice.

The states' transition from institutional to welfare to administrative stages, is a mark of civil meltdown[2]—a devolutionary reality. Individual–environmental bondages cannot remain hinged at a time when societal bonds of legitimacy are broken. *Age-old social practice outcomes become counter-functional as their lost legitimacy begins to masquerade as a surrogate-helper.*

From Homer, Plato, Aristotle to Kafka and Albert Camus, *Sisyphus* has been embedded in social reality. Human aspirations, struggles, conquests and falls underscore a Sisyphean condition that defines futility, courage and revolt in search of a meaning. Is that the *will* to struggle and survive?

If there were no social problems, there would not have been a need for SW. It does not mean SW's existence would pre-empt the prevalence of social problems. The obvious implication is that *problem, policy and practice* constitute a cycle of hope against hope since human existence is trapped in an absurd quest for happiness in an inherently unjust world. I theorize that *social work* was invented as a detour to a goal that was inherently unclear at best. This formulation posits itself as a blasphemy to the flat-earthers of current theory and practice of SW.

We created social institutions and arrangements with a hybrid philosophy of naïveté and arrogance. The consequence is, both in

---

[2] https://www.nytimes.com/2017/03/07/world/europe/wikileaks-cia-hacking. html?emc=edit_na_20170307&nl=breaking-news&nlid=72603810&ref=headline (accessed on 7 March 2017).

the US, India and elsewhere, unmitigated social–personal problems ranging from terrorism to adolescent depression, on one hand, and racism, sexism and the like, on the other, persist. Consequently, we confront a situation filled with varied meltdowns: institutional, economic, social, political and cultural.

While no earth-shaking catastrophic vision is presupposed here, a compounded crisis of confidence, character and credibility looms large on the horizon; it pales in the fog of insecurity, inertia and ideology. Paradoxically, credible techno-scientific advancements, global connectedness and the 'rise of the rest' marks a significant epoch in the evolution of this civilization.[3]

Human race confronts evolutionary contradictions. A capacity to self-annihilation is not evolutionary. Devolution is markedly visible when *success of progress* is critically examined. It seems self-destructive trappings are innate and a mega crisis is imminent. Our subconscious neglect of this realization is congruent with human nature.

Psychoanalytic positivism is both *denial of death* and 'quest for immortality' (1973) which led to the 'practice of cryonics'. The new *crisis of legitimacy* rests on three basic postulates: (a) functionality, (b) authenticity and (c) credibility.

Scientists have successfully achieved the state of editing DNA genes, which amounts to recoding the life of humans. In other words, it is a rational substitution of God. Is there a comparable accomplishment in social sciences? Is social science an oxymoron? Work per se did not exist without 'social'. Contemporary society warrants a new classificatory system to establish congruent reality.

---

[3] 'The philosopher Richard Taylor uses the myth of Sisyphus as a representation of a life made meaningless because it consists of bare repetition. James Clement van Pelt, co-founder of Yale's Initiative in Religion, Science & Technology suggests that Sisyphus also personifies humanity and its disastrous pursuit of perfection by any means necessary, in which the great rock repeatedly rushing down the mount symbolizes the accelerating pace of unsustainable civilization toward cataclysmic collapse and cultural oblivion that ends each historical age and restarts the Sisyphean cycle'. https://en.wikipedia.org/wiki/Sisyphus (accessed on 5 November 2016).

Social sciences have inherent limitations. The recognition of this fact is academic humility. The denial of this reality is both hubris and malpractice. No other discipline or professional area is guiltier of this cardinal sin than SW and its cognate academic aspects mainly inclusive of social welfare, social policy, social development, 'clinical social work', counselling and related subjects. Its pervasive inclusivity from 'casework' to 'military social work' deprives it of a designated identity. You name any problem and field, it is an acceptable prefix to 'social work'.

Poverty of Culture, Diversity and Policy Paralysis

Race, gender and class have universally stratified societies in culturally structured systems of inequality. Innuendoes, stereotypes and prejudices have simply justified varied forms of 'blame-the-victim' doctrines which abound in American academia. Even *diversity*—its enigma and politics—have become counterproductive.[4] 'There is something perverse about a notion of diversity that would require us to treat Asian-American excellence as a confounding variable to be (partially) corrected for, rather than a legacy to be celebrated', writes Kelefa Sanneh, a critic at large, in *The New Yorker* (2017). Noting the limits of 'diversity', Sanneh concludes, 'Where affirmative action was about compensatory justice, diversity is meant to be a shared benefit. But does the rationale carry weight?'

'Culture of poverty', I have contended, has perpetuated the myths that serve as surrogates of status quo. Basic *public* and *social* policy debates and programme structures are formulated, designed and operationalized on the explicit notions that sustain this dubious rationale (Mohan 2011).

---

[4] I prefer 'inclusive' to 'diversity' since the latter appears to be less than non-discriminatory. https://www.newyorker.com/magazine/2017/10/09/the-limits-of-diversity?mbid=social_google%2B (accessed on 5 December 2017).

The current US administration unravels keen understanding of the dynamics of 'basket of deplorables' aka 'white trash'.[5] No other phrase has so succinctly, albeit subconsciously, conveyed the hidden demons of this American democracy than Hillary Clinton's brutally honest characterization of the poor whites in America. There is a chimeric quality underlying social programmes that characterize the poor and helpless as victims of their own subhuman traits rather than holding the actual perpetrators of injustice responsible for inbuilt systemic inhumanity.

Partisan factionalism organized around founding fathers—John Adams, Alexander Hamilton, Thomas Jefferson and Aaron Burr—is ingrained in the DNA of America's political evolution as a democracy (Blumenthal 2016: 39). 'Adams had entered the presidency in 1797 professing his "positive passion for public good".... [yet he] demanded deference to hierarchy and class, was contemptuous of new forms of political democracy', writes Sidney Blumenthal (2016: 38).

The presidential campaigns in 2016 marked a new low in public discourse. The ferocity of digital–social media simply added fuel to the fire of hyper-populism, hypocrisies and politically incorrect rhetoric and realties.

The only iron law in public policy is that there is no law in this complex domain. Institutions prevail; interest groups play games and incremental changes persist despite radical slogans. The transformation is neither linear nor bilinear; it is a regressive–liberal pendulum that suits the ruling elites. If William Epstein (2017) is correct, masses rule in democracy and elites need them to sustain their power. In a cynical circular manner, they both suffer from a false consciousness of power.

Faith, guilt and fear usually push the wheels of social change. Ideologies did not come until belief systems were crystalized along personalities and dogmas of people in quest of power. Such vehicles never go in purportedly one direction. What we find globally, regressive–progressive change is the rule rather than exception. The classless

---

[5] https://www.academia.edu/30607909/White_trash_in_the_basket_of_deplorables_continued_crisis_of_men_in_America (accessed on 24 July 2017).

societies envisioned by Stalin and Mao brought back horrors of past mayhem and oppression. The current situation is not much different. What they call 'fourth revolution' is actually a counter-revolution.

The God That Failed

Do not be proud, but be willing to associate with people of low position. Do not be conceited.
    —Romans 12:16 [New International Version (NIV)].

'And the prayer of faith will save the one who is sick' (James 5:15). Much of charity- and faith-based SP is an outcome of this Judeo–Christian morality. Most world religions follow similar convictions. Classic altruism sustains a dysfunctional system of self-regulated functionality.

The demise of civility and near full control by techno-political enterprises and a feckless revolt of the masses have lead us to a level when megalomaniacs, criminals and mindless leaders pervert public and social policy. Race, gender and class—not exactly in the same order—have divided human family since times immemorial. The postmodern political correctness simply offshoots marginalization driven by an interest-group campaign that borders on orthodoxy. Contemporary SW as 'professed' and 'practised' today in America and overseas is a manifestation of this unexamined theorizing.

Tons of SW textbooks have flooded commercial bookstores. The drivers of this academic mercantilism are so-called intellectuals and educators who hold tenured positions and run CSWE, National Association of Social Workers (NASW), International Consortium for Social Development and, lately, the American Academy of Social Work and Social Welfare (AASWSW). Pervasive institutional *narcissism* and interests perpetuate a nearly incestuous anti-intellectual culture that serves its own trappings in the name of professional advancement.

A closer examination would unravel certain existential fissures that compound the crisis of social work education, practice and research (SW-EPR). The author studied this formulation in *Logic of Social*

Welfare and proposed an epistemologically sound alternate discipline in 'Social Praxeology' (Mohan 1988, Chapter IV: 61–71). It did not get much traction. Cognitive dissonance warrants reflective consciousness.

An evaluative perusal reveals: (a) Modern SW is an American innovation. But the post-American century is vastly different in nature. Globalization of democracy (and SW) internationalized some values and practices without resolving global–social issues. And (b) strategies to resolve complex social problems, knowing full well SW's inanity and limits, amount to professional practice of *bad faith*.

The Human–Social Development

Human reality in the age of nihilist terror is only compounded by the silent echoes of helplessness. Help!!!

As the paradox of postmodernity unfolds, angst and alienation deepen. Hannah Arendt could not have imagined why fanatics would kill *Charlie Hebdo* in Paris and Buddhist monks kill Muslims in Myanmar. Building on Sartrean phenomenology, Foucauldian archaeology (of knowledge) and my own 2 cents, I seek to revisit a theory of human–social development (HSD) that might make some sense in an otherwise confused state of knowledge.

SD is an ineffectual surrogate of international SW. HSD perspective is a key to understand the existential crisis: *Trappings of human nature call for a unified science to unravel the HSD paradox.* SW and SD are failed modalities of change in the face of a deeper malaise. In a climate of social meltdowns, humans ask for more than 'social'.

CHAPTER 5

Transforming Social Work[1]

...[M]an could avoid the fate of a Welfare-Through-Warfare State only by achieving a new starting point where he could reconstruct the productive apparatus without that 'inner worldly asceticism' which provided the mental basis for domination and exploration.
—Herbert Marcuse (1966: xiv).

'Transforming Social Work' is a reflective analysis of our profession that stands at the crossroads of change in a globally transformed world. While basic societal institutions falter, individual, family and community strive for functional sustainability. The status, legitimacy and need of a professional discipline can only be sustained if the structure of a profession is organized in congruence with cultural, social, economic and political realties embedded in the forces of change.

This thematic address seeks to examine three basic aspects of professional consequence: *mission* of SW; *educational* infrastructure

[1] This chapter is partly based on my keynote address delivered in honour of S. Zafar Hasan, my mentor, friend and guide, at the 3rd National Indian Social Work Congress, 24–26 October 2015, titled 'Community Engagement, Social Responsibility and Social Work Profession' at Jain Vishwa Bharti Institute, Ladnun, Rajasthan, India [jointly sponsored by National Association of Professional Social Workers in India (NAPSWI)].

and *service* aspects of its delivery, research, funding and values. These stances differ from much of what we know about and do in SW within and beyond educational settings. A critical examination unravels concerns that merit attention of the professional community to adapt to and align with realities that dictate *transformative practice* to achieving sustainable peace, prosperity and progress in a global community. SP—an alternative to contemporary SW—is proffered as an epistemologically sound and aesthetically unified framework.

We are on the cusp of a new techno-global revolution that is transforming the human family with unthinkable, unintended consequences. The digital interface with economy, production and management of resources has created smoke and screens amidst daunting challenges. Our greatest challenge today is to devise policy mechanisms that can sustain a viable equilibrium of human and social development.

Costas Douzinas, a political philosopher, raised a seminal question: 'Is there an intrinsic relationship between human rights and the recent wars carried out in their name? Are human rights a barrier against domination and oppression, or the ideological gloss of an emerging empire?' (2007). Douzinas examines the paradox of a contemporary humanitarianism that has abandoned politics in favour of combating evil (Douzinas 2000).

> Cosmopolitanism is the formal ideology of the new order; the removal of violence and perpetual peace its alleged end. But insofar as wars, violence and torture are its modus operandi, human rights now codify and 'constitutionalize' the normative sources of empire. While the sovereignty of states and the territorial principle have been weakened, no sense of world community has developed. (Douzinas 2007)

Douzinas concludes, 'it is precisely the renewal of an ancient cosmopolitanism that may give rise to a new politics of community' (2007). I contextualize 'community' in a wider context to examine how humanitarian endeavours are impacting social services and what are its implied ramifications for people who depend on structures of help.

If Sisyphus were an optimist—a counterfactual supposition, I guess—pushing, mindlessly, rocks up the hill might have had some point.

The *absurdity* of life, however, leaves all mortals to carry the burdensome 'rocks' in the name of karma and/or dharma. SW looks like a Sisyphean occupation. I quote Richard Taylor:

> Each man's life thus resembles one of Sisyphus's climbs to the summit of his hill and each day of it one of his steps; the difference is that whereas Sisyphus himself returns to push the stone up again, we leave this to our children. (1970: 263)

This collective human strife is a universal drama of existence punctuated by occasional protest. The very act of transformation is a revolt. Are we there yet? Or do we stand compromised for good?

Humankind and social misery are twins. Else, Siddhartha would not have become the Buddha. Social workers today confront a dilemma that calls for resolution in a very complex world.

The 'great fall of China' and India's 'caste, creed, and conflict' (*The Economist* 2015) will not much change where almost one-third of humanity resides. Yet, things must change beyond simple infrastructural cosmetics.

In the digital age, altruism is defined by the analytics of human behaviour that determine individual motivation, choices and cultural trends. Certain algorithms will replace what service providers and provision allocators have done during the entire twentieth century. At the turn of century, it is time to rethink the purpose and method of SW that has marginally contributed to mitigate unwarranted suffering.

The framework that I submit here posits a synthesis of five unifying principles, which I consider basic to SW and SP.[2]

A New Framework: Mission, Education and Service

A profession that does not innovate tends to devolve. A profession without clear vision is a ship without a compass and radar. A discipline

---

[2] I use SW and SP quite interchangeably. However, the burden of this chapter is to signify evolutionary transformation of SW to SP as a logical outcome.

without authentic knowledge base is like a runaway train destined to crash. And any service organization without effective, demonstrable outcome indices is akin to a vehicle that has misaligned wheels around a loose axis. In a world changed by a few simple algorithms, there is no room for inefficiency, ineffectiveness and inanity. SW, despite its emergence as a profession during the last hundred years or so, still remains an incomplete profession without a clear mission, credible knowledge base and authentic record of effectiveness.

The purpose of SW has always been to humanize systems of assistance at individual, family, group, community and societal levels. Professionalization of benevolence is an act of civilizational guilt. Since culture progresses at the expense of *Eros,* it becomes eventually self-destructive (Freud 1949: 122). Loss of *innocence* is perhaps the deadliest achievement of our civilization.

SW developed specialized methods and generalist interventions as modalities to extend professional 'help' at different levels of system.

India has a unique role to universalize SW. Yes, it takes a village to raise a child. It takes a nation to nurture and develop villages that incubate healthy childhoods. Few years ago, I went to visit my grand-father's village near Mursan, my hometown near Mathura. I saw a few signs of progress—a small primary school, a bridge over rivulet Karvan and an old mango tree—but there was hardly a man visible. Desolate rural areas, without much social-developmental protection, are mostly populated by single, uneducated mothers without physical presence of a male provider who still remains the cornerstone of a patricentric-territorial-acquisitive culture.

The *fallacies of development* (Mohan 2007) are written all over like graffiti in a rundown neighbourhood of Detroit—a dying city that once stood as the emblematic engine of American productivity and capitalism. With due regards, I am not too overwhelmed by a French economist (Picketty 2014) or a papal homily that underscore the importance of equality and justice in a dangerously unequal world.

The pursuit of knowledge is truth, not perfection. From Rigveda to Rwanda—as social archaeology unravels—one finds the footprints of a creature that can hide his claws under the disguise of a leader (Mohan 2015a). Analytics, statistics and methodologies of research are tools of a process. SW's knowledge base has been confounded by twentieth-century conceptions and contradictions of causal relationships.

I think post-war emergence of the Welfare State served as a Trojan horse to justify its offensive against the spectre of communism and socialism. As post-War economies and politics unfolded, institutional 'developmentalism' evolved as a new messiah to extend public services to counteract insecurities and contingencies. The functionaries, which operated this complex machine, are today's social and public policymakers, social welfare theorists and social workers.

The end of the cold war, fall of the Berlin Wall, information revolution, globalized democracy and digital power fundamentally changed the calculus of life within and beyond national boundaries. The rise of Chinese hybrid economy, inexplicable fundamentalism and the anti-state ISIS—not to mention the ubiquitous fear of domestic and international terrorism—demonstrably alert the risks of new patterns of intersocietal relationships. In the confluence of these contrapuntal forces, it is unwise at best to follow a particular model of social policies and services. It partakes of special significance when the Welfare State is in deep crisis. Populism can use this dying institution but the state has neither will nor resources to sustain it. Social workers serve as ineffectual angels with a schizophrenic personality. They are unwittingly trapped in a no-win situation.

Rhetorically an altruistic occupation committed to equality and justice, SW embodied the idealism of Judeo-Christian values. In reality, its glorious façade did succeed in hiding the persistence of poverty, racism and injustice without substantially transforming the root causes of social misery and economic doldrums. Our knowledge base lacks philosophically grounded scientific mythologies that would mitigate the genesis of despair.

Social work research (SWR) maintained a shallow positivistic camouflage to sustain a functionalist ideology that runs counter to any of its avowed humanistic goals. Its rise and fall is reflective of the politics of social services devised to thwart social upheaval. As models of Western democracies influenced the rising democracies growing out of the colonial slumber in the developing nations, the American model of SW education and practice became the dominant exemplar for rest of the world.

In the post-American world, the lingering issues—legitimacy, effectiveness and credibility—come close to its Achilles heel. From 'single case study design' to its strength–capacity–competency–resiliency-based approaches to 'problem-solving', the methodological aspects of its research domain remain painfully weak. SWR has hardly found its niche in the realm of social sciences.

A few schools equipped with institutional prowess have acquired funded research centres, which employ investigators usually for survey research and investigations that support graduate students and faculty summer stipends with reduced workload. Lesser programmes are either coalesced with vocational divisions or nearly eliminated as unsustainable units. In sum, SW's current status as an academically, philosophically well-grounded profession is hard to sustain. Its foundation as a discipline seems rather weak at best and parasitic at worst.

In *The Logic of Social Welfare*, more than 25 years ago, I conceptualized SW whole within a SW-EPR framework (Mohan 1988). I had rationalized 'Social Praxeology' as a preferred name substituting 'Social Work'. I revisit this issue here and conceptualize SP as a viable alternate.

As I examine current realties in the global context, I believe we must professionally underscore three foci: mission, education and service. In other words, MES ought to replace SW-EPR. There are sound reasons in support of this unified whole (to be elaborated later in this presentation).

The Context and Complexity

SW education has proliferated in most of the countries including Eastern Europe, Latin America, China and other South Asian and African countries. While graduate programmes are still confined to

America, Canada, Australia and India, undergraduate studies are flourishing. Although governmental ministries and institutional statutes regulate their organization and standards, their accrediting procedures and agencies do not conform to any particular model. Education, training, fieldwork and curricular designs, however, seem to emulate the American model.

It is my contention that the American model of SW education is dated and does not meet the challenges of changing global realities. Aping this twentieth-century design does not logically suit the needs of a dynamic society anywhere. The dualities of East and West and polarities of North and South do not correspond to globalized challenges. A profession that does not naturally evolve gets choked off and remains developmentally challenged.

The contours of a new techno-digital society have fundamentally changed the nature of human interactions, economic productivity and social values that bind us together as global family. It is crucial to comprehend the design and structure of this *brave new world*. All HSD processes are in a state of flux at the moment.

Violence is an American pie. Likewise, India's dharma. The cult of violence and rapaciously garish consumerism has nearly destroyed the innate values and age-old ethical standards of our day-to-day conduct in the land of Buddha and Gandhi. The 'professional' execution of a scholarly thinker in Delhi retards the progress on the road to civility. 'So who killed Malleshappa Kalburgi, a leading Indian scholar and a well-known rationalist thinker'?[3]

SW education cannot be studied in isolation. Compunctions of a pseudo-industrial–democratic society rising from centuries-old repression of colonial rule—evidently South Asia in this context—apparently liberate people from their tabooistic culture unleashing untapped libidinal energy in the seductive environment of their gentrified environment. But the ones uprooted from their rural habitat to help develop new islands of prosperity are seldom allowed economic

[3] http://www.bbc.com/news/world-asia-india-34105187?SThisFB (accessed on 5 September 2015).

equality in an unjust society. 'Certainly there can be "pleasure" in alienated labor too' (Marcuse 1966: 220).

Displaced masses in and around New Delhi, Mumbai or any other growing metropolis—often homeless living under cheap plastic canopies far away from the neon lights of prosperity—cannot protest, let alone revolt. A few of their young and restless do often become rapists and killers—new man-eaters of Kumaon avenging their hunters!—making ugly headlines in media. No casework, therapy, community organization and SWR can stop this monstrously complex *developmentality*.[4]

Techno–digital society cuts through the hierarchized layers of 'patricentric-acquisitive' (Marcuse 1966: 241) culture. It cannibalizes time; virtual reality bums into human reality. It offers instant gratification, the hallmark of new hedonism promoting a 'hangout' culture shattering the age-old taboos and redefining 'family', 'marriage' and 'community'—the pivotal institutions of our civilization. In the United States, nearly 45 per cent children are born to single mothers; the rate of divorce, even amongst seniors, is staggering.

Having lived more than half of my life—1 March 1975 to date—in the United States of America, I have come to realize unfortunate persistence of Darwinian forces that sustain social atavism. Liberal democracies attained limited success to promote economic growth, which helped the rise of middle class consumerism. But no one is really concerned about the fate of the poor. In presidential debates as well as state-of-the-union addresses, I only hear about commitments to the middle class. What happened to the 'underclass' of the pre-Reagan–Thatcher era? Today, the gulf between poor and the rich—and consequential rise of inequality and economic injustice—is higher in the Western democracies. No wonder 'democracies of unfreedom' (Mohan 1966) are the world's largest democracies.

Pope Francis delivered his homily in the Revolutions Square, Havana, in the backdrop of Che Guevara's looming portrait.

---

[4] A theory I developed to show how counter-development is causing social meltdowns (Mohan 2015b).

His sermon invoked the Christian ideal of service: 'Service is never ideological for we do not serve ideas. We serve people'.[5] Ideology is inbuilt in the design of all faith-based, philanthropic, altruistic modalities delivered in varied benevolent attires. We need independent productive people in and around healthy families and communities to build a cohesive but diverse society wedded to tolerance and nonviolent modes of conflict resolution. This goal is thwarted by a host of atavistic forces that impede progress.

Revolt of the *Aam Aadmi* (common man) in Delhi, India shook the foundations of the establishment. The much-heralded leadership failed the masses. Delhi is a microcosm of India, but it is not India. The real India still lies where farmers commit suicides; innocent children are enslaved; girls are raped; minorities are terrorized; criminal politicians rule; reactionaries of abominable politics thrive; political correctness becomes dysfunctional; brown bureaucrats ape the white colonial rulers; and Buddha and Gandhi play mascots of nonviolence in which no one—yes, no one!—believes. India, the world's largest democracy, presents a bewildering panorama of complex corruption, staggering inefficiency and heartless mendacity.

Are these problems merely social? A feudal–colonial drama that spans over ten centuries posits culture that succumbed to its own follies, frailties and flaws. Darwin wins. Marx fails. Gandhi becomes a footnote to history.

I believe no populist revolt solves any problem. Each revolution has been followed by authoritarianism. All our gods have failed us. However, it is not 'the god who failed us'; it is our own sad acquiescence and unprincipled passive–aggressive reflexes that brought us down from the accomplished helm to the self-coveted hell. A 'community' cannot coexist with casteism, communalism and public corruption.

Family, community, society and *responsibility* are social constructs. The demise of 'social'—if real—is the greatest tragedy of the much-hyped twenty-first century.

---

[5] http://www.nytimes.com/2015/09/21/world/americas/pope-francis-cuba. html?_r=0 (accessed on 22 September 2015).

Our 'gated-communities' vitiate the spirit of 'community'. The nuclear family that Talcott Parsons defined is dead. The concept of community is a romantic myth. When basic social–economic institutions fail, family and community cease as a primary incubator of cohesiveness and solidarity.

Community health may be threatened without positive 'communal motivation'[6] (Bleyer 2015: 43). Unfortunately, however, communalism —a moral equivalent of racism in America—has come to embody the most explosive and nefarious experiences of civil existence in India. We live in segregated sectors imprisoned in the hierarchies of race and class. These new structures of day-to-day life develop new mores of living that violate the very principles of community organization.

Social responsibility is a rhetorical concept in a culture that values disvalues in reality. It is not India's misfortune alone. It characterizes our material-territorial civilization. Individuals, groups and communities at large tend to seek survival in self-interests. Contemporary SW's matricentric-acquisitive territoriality is no less troubling. We study and teach outdated subjects which have no reality orientation. Do the rulers of this country practise social responsibility?

There is hardly an opportunity to actualize social responsibility in an irresponsible society. The naked reality stinks—uncollected garbage, your nextdoor neighbour urinating in front of your house, deliberately unleashed hoard of pigs scavenging ubiquitously, not to mention a mass psychosis of public corruption—as soon as you step out of your home.

Whenever I visit India, I do see fragments of change underway. There is a metro-tube service in New Delhi. A few other cities are working to improve infrastructural facilities. But does it take six decades to realize that working men and women of this vast nation deserve a measure of public transportation?

---

[6] I am applying this concept beyond microlevel. Community is an extension of primary relationships on a wider level. If partners in bed can help each other with 'communal motivation' (Bleyer 2015: 42–43), communitarians can also rebuild fractured relationships. What has happened in Ferguson, MS in the USA should alert policymakers and social planners everywhere.

From overpopulation to hygienic horrors to national security, we blame a particular religious minority for our social and political miseries. It is too late to blame Gandhi, Jinnah and Nehru for the partition of *matribhumi* (motherland). The ghosts of a colonially structured country haunt modest possibilities of developmental projects that fail to deliver.

Social Practice: A Paradigm Shift[7]

> The new global conflict—post-ideological nihilism—is essentially a meltdown of the existing social contract. A veritable dystopia has virtually replaced the twentieth-century scenarios of hope. Human-made catastrophes and natural disasters further compound the challenges that scientists, philosophers, policymakers and social engineers must confront in these troubled times. (Mohan 2011: 145)

The 'end of work' (Thompson 2015) is no scientific fiction. The 'future of work' has become a lucrative business.[8] A few simple algorithms have changed the world we live in. We will not have SW as defined, offered and practised today. There are protests against university closures of SW departments in the United Kingdom. Schools of SW are being downgraded as departmental units in colleges that are less than academic or central to institutional missions.

This crisis of SW is not new. Manifestations become reality when 'rubber hits the road'. The legitimacy of SW as a profession (Mohan 1988: Chapter IV) continues. My approach to *social practice* is designed to unify the art and science of social praxis, HSD and global welfare.

Unification of social work implies symbiosis of facts and values (Mohan 1999). Contemporary scientific advancements and techno-logical strides bluntly reject the premise and purpose of SW offered mainly on the tenets of Western Judeo–Christian mythologies.

---

[7] Based on my lecture delivered to Retired Social Workers of LA, 214 Ag Center, LSU, 7 August 2015. http://www.brijmohan.org/2RSWLecAug2015.pdf (accessed on 5 December 2017).

[8] https://summit.presidents.eu/summit (accessed on 15 August 2017).

Buddha, Nietzsche, Kabir, Gandhi and Confucius cannot be ignored in a complexly integrated yet divided post-American world. The lingering dualities of the past call for a funeral of the decadent past. A paradigm shift is called for *unification* rather than fragmentation and convenient conflicts.

A new fulcrum of course offering synthesizing humanities, arts and sciences undergirds social *practice* as a new vehicle of social transformation involving empirical, anecdotal, objective–subjective resources to authenticate a new perspective and its validity to salvage the profession from its own inanity and irrelevance. As an innovative and substantially different approach, *social practice* becomes a unified realm for all academics, social scientists, policymakers, students and people who are committed to root out unmitigated human suffering. SP thus posits itself as an academic calling rather than a career path with a meaningless *licence to practise.*

Rationale in support of this approach include (a) relative transparency and accountability, (b) aesthetic–axiological appeal and (c) dynamic synthesis of Western and Eastern values, reality and reason. *Unification* of science and humanities is a work in progress; departmental cries for 'autonomy' is a lost cause. University structure and function, likewise, warrants a radical change in orientation and purpose.

The revenants of Freud and Marx are back. The 'individual' that Sigmund Freud invented sought Marxian support as the industrial revolution and wars destroyed his/her personality. The Welfare State is in crisis. From cradle to grave protection is history. The best educated, most talented people do not have any retirement system. In academia, 'tenure track' has become 'tenure trap' breeding mediocrity, nepotism and abuse of power by a privileged few.

Seven pillars, metaphorically, constitute a fulcrum of certain metavalues that underscore the unification of knowledge, skills and practice. Chapter 7 is a small ladder to reach these goals.

CHAPTER 6

Hermeneutics of Help

Too many researchers have learned in methods courses that the aim of science is to discover universal laws, and the method is to deduce causal hypotheses from more general theories and test them against masses of observable data. This teaching has had dogmatic certitude—that's what science is; philosophers of science say so, and they know—that has not been present in many of the logical empiricists themselves.

—Paul Diesing (1991: x).

One of the main premises of this book is: *Help* as a social construct validates charity and philanthropy as universal altruism. Human instincts imply pleasure and pain. The notion of seven pillars of SP proffered here involve small steps relative to (a) altruism and help, (b) science and social science and (c) social hope. It is my endeavour to explain how these core tenets can bring about basic changes in the existing epistemologies of 'help'.

Altruism, Help and Hubris[1]

'Hermeneutics deal with clarifying the meaning of text, and by extension the meaning of any human action, product, or expression

---

[1] Parts of this section are based on Chapter I of my book (2015b: 3–30). I am grateful to Palgrave Macmillan, NY for their understanding to let me use these comments in the interest of professional collaboration in search for global well-being.

that can be treated as a text' (Diesing 1991: 105). The *practice* of social sciences cannot be value-free.

Licensing of qualified *practice* implies qualified 'objective' review and impartial certification. In SW, this *practice* has been implemented lately. This definition is broadly vague and their review process is political. As defined and reviewed by Louisiana Board of Social Work Education, I am not a 'social work' educator who can teach even social policy:

> Who is required to have a social work credential issued by the Board? Any individual with a degree in social work either at the undergraduate or graduate level that is practicing social work in Louisiana. Social work practice is the professional application of social work values, theories, and interventions to one or more of the following: enhancing the development, problem-solving, and coping capacities of people; promoting the effective and humane operations of systems that provide resources and services to people; linking people with systems that provide them with resources, services, and opportunities; developing and improving social policy; and engaging in research related to the professional activities.
>
> The practice of social work includes but is not limited to clinical social work, planning and community organization, policy and administration, research, and social work education.[2]

Ira Colby, a prominent SW educator and administrator, wrote 'Challenging Social Work Education's Urban Legends' in the *Journal of Social Work Education* (2014: 216–219). Myths and critical reasoning are hostile to each other. Our notion of 'help'—the hallmark of SW—is based on the mythologies of altruistic latter-day folklores. With

---

[2] http://www.labswe.org (accessed on 12 August 2014). By this definition, I must have their so-called 'licence' to write and teach anything, let alone 'practice' SW. This clearly violates my freedom as a Dean Emeritus (Social Work, LSU), a US citizen as well as a 'Social Work Pioneer' (NASW 1995). As I saw the local politics in Louisiana in the mid-1990s, the advocates this pernicious law meant to achieve two regressive objectives: (a) unburden unproductive social work faculty to conduct research and publish and (b) exclude scholarly intellectuals.

reference to Ira Colby's take on 'urban legends' (2014: 216–219), I submit a few observations for public discourse. The Colby conclusion is worth a note:

> A rigorous questioning of our legends may determine that some are appropriate, whereas others are misguided. However, the validation of education models and resulting policies based on *philosophical or ideological perspectives*, which are *void of evidence-based driven critical thinking* processes, will ultimately lead to *the irrelevancy of professional social work education*. As social work educators, we must challenge the many legends and traditions that drive our longstanding beliefs. To do otherwise only permanently cements social work education's place as *being extraneous in the eyes of the broader academic community*. (2014: 206–217; emphasis added)

These findings in our flagship journal embody conflicts, concerns and contradictions in a century-old 'profession' that is still searching for its soul amidst the madness of orthodoxies and fads supported by scientific method. I shall confine my critique to the highlighted expressions in the excerpt just quoted.

It is a fallacious contention that philosophical–ideological orientations are scientifically unsound. SW itself is founded on the tenets of Judeo-Christian belief systems.

Critical thinking is a quintessential element of postmodern philosophical tradition largely owed to Nietzsche, Marx and Freud. Colby's attempt to dichotomize philosophy and science is misguided.

SW's irrelevancy is self-deserved. We all became second-class citizens due to our own 'institutional–individual narcissism'. Our raw careerism and unprincipled, unsubstantiated rhetoric of diversity and social justice simply fast-tracked this process.

'Evidence-based driven' methodology as postulated amounts to a delusion in a field that remains parasitic at best. Evaluative processes including programme reviews, reaffirmation of accreditation, scholarly peer reviews and promotion–tenure standards are fraught with questionable policies, practices and procedures. Self-renewal is in fact self-preservation.

When impending downgrading of the School of Social Work lately occurred at the LSU, I advocated to get it incorporated into the College of Humanities and Social Sciences. Unfortunately, my own school preferred to align with softer disciplines, human ecology, library, education and the like. The professoriate in power chose the latter for obvious 'unscientific' convenience.

I consider myself to be a humanist, educator and social scientist. Alas, I was lonely in this strife. Our school chose to become a part of *College of Human Sciences and Education* for very pragmatic reasons. Speaking of 'human sciences', how many of us really teach, understand and practise Foucauldian theories? The truth is self-evident. Having worked tirelessly over half a century in the field, I feel SW has become its own nemesis.[3]

Gary Becker was a 'real-world economist' (*Time* 2014, May 19: 21). Lawrence Summers writes, 'If...economics is an imperial social science, Gary Becker was its emperor' (*Time* 2014, May 19: 21). There has never been a Gary Becker in social welfare and/or social work. SW's alleged imperialism is a subconscious self-glorification that some international scholars disingenuously invoked to cash off at the expense of the profession itself.

Theory and Social Work

There have been feckless debates whether SW needs a theory or not. In a way, SW is an applied amalgamation of many theories that need validation or refutation. As William Epstein would say: 'It's all a romance'. A theory of theories does not exist in social sciences. As examined in the pages that follow, 'political and social development' got embedded in the social system as a functional expedience. Norman Birnbaum sums this up rather brilliantly:

> Above all, the world's difficulties were attributed to the unequal rate of a process termed 'modernization,' which, when completed,

---

[3] http://www.tandfonline.com/doi/full/10.1080/10437797.2014.947167 (accessed on 24 September 2015).

would complete its pacification. Behind much of this lay, of course, two convictions. One was that the American model of political and social development was canonical, especially the model provided by the New Deal and Keynesian Welfare State. The second was that domination, relationships of power could be domesticated— no—nullified. This was a projection onto the globe of what was current in academia, a systematic denial of the structure of power in the United States. (Birnbaum 1988: 333)

Parsonsian social system (and action) goes beyond nullification; it amounts to justification so that a possible state of imbalances is never reached. His theory of social action, as examined later, is a cornerstone of a Welfare State that simplifies inequality as a systemic karma. 'In a way, every social theory is a discreet obituary or celebration for some social system', wrote Alvin Gouldner (1970: 47). The demise of social theory is understandably attributable to systemic meltdowns despite elaborate theoretical 'infrastructure'.

There is a phalanx of Nobel laureates in economics and none can account for the rise of 1 per cent (richest elites) in a country based on the premise of liberty, equality and justice. Individual, family, community, society and culture are going through a crisis of conscience that belies any theoretical basis. Anomie? Anarchy? Systemic failures cannot be theorized without deeper, deconstructive analytics of historico-cultural forces. In a current movie based on Lois Lowry's bestseller *The Giver*, one cannot escape cultural self-destruction in the name of progress. Is the culture of contemporary SW really progressive? Expedient liberalism is a negation of principled progress.

Archaeology, a historiographical method as developed by Michel Foucault in his groundbreaking studies *Madness and Civilization* (1965 [1988]), *The Birth of the Clinic* (1973[1994]), *The Order of Things* (1970[1994]) and *The Archaeology of Knowledge* (1969[1972]), refers to discursive consciousness involving discourses on ideas—episteme— that go beyond rules, domains, structures and language. 'Social Work is a helping profession'—is a benign but hollow statement without much substance and discursive relevance. There is hardly a human enterprise which is not 'social' and 'helping'.

Archaeology of a profession would involve a meaningful organization of formulations of 'help' that qualifies a particular set of attributes of 'social work'. *Social practice* is thus a more dynamic realm of archaeological exploration when it comes to analyzing human–social interactions relative to each other's issues and problems while attempting a meaningful discourse.

The reduction of SW from a helping, altruistic profession to a self-serving, marketplace career apparently amounts to a derivation what Ernest Nagel called 'deductive-nomological model' (1961: 361) where one scientific theory from another is unified in terms of basic laws. Since SW as such remains unsupported by any rigorous scientific basis, Nagel's reasoning cannot be applied here. In other words, it is neither derivation nor evolution; it is devolution that is at work.

Foucauldian discourse on SW—to use Gilles Deleuze's words—thus involves 'theory–practice of multiplicities' that meaningfully employs theories and constructs involving power, language and relationships including various worldviews, ideologies, values and their politics as illustrated later by Jacques Derrida's deconstruction and critical theory. SW is a poorly baptized professional identity. On the contrary, if I may:

SP, historiographically, is a knowledge-based application of benevolence toward the annihilation of dehumanizing forces that thwart HSD and promote alienation and oppression.

To substantiate my contention, a critical appraisal of important Foucauldian formulations will be helpful at the outset. His 'history of ideas' involves linear perspectives on history and 'epistemes'. His emphasis has been power structures that unravel madness, civilization, clinic, human sexuality and sciences. SW's proclivities are inversely related to his discursive, deconstructive and emancipatory emphases.

From its antiquity, philanthropic altruism and humanitarian concerns have propelled individuals and communities to use charity as the principal mode of service to the poor and the needy. Such impulses have served as a cover to hide societal–institutional injustices that breed human misery. Western interventions used Judeo-Christian values to offer the same protection ensuring the dominance of organized religion in the lives of oppressed people. What karma and dharma achieved in the Vedic (Hindu) culture—institutionalized inequality without any recourse to justice in the current life—Western orthodoxies, beginning eighteenth century, practised more formally under the shadows of commandments, subsequently, recast as *Enlightenment.*

With the 'birth of clinic', *clients* came into the realm of 'practice'. Twentieth century's post-War effects changed the mode of 'practice'. *Clientization* in SWP is an outcome of modelling medical and legal practices. A therapeutic society needs caretakers especially when primary institutions and bonds fall apart.

Professionally delivered—privately or publicly—services to individuals, families, groups and communities fall within the realm of SW. However, the focus has shifted from community to individuals. This may be attributable to many a factor: change in ideology, rise of therapeutic industry and regression of public and social policies.

SP per se does not exist in professional parlance and literature. Excepting a book on research (Diesing 1991), I have not come across it as a worthwhile construct though continental social theory is replete with numerous references. I see, *social practice,* as a transformative exercise of existential hope, that is, persistent search for freedom (Mohan 2003). This outlook is qualitatively different than contemporary theories and practices of SW. The 'theory of social work' is essentially miscegenation of selected social and psychological perspectives on human functions. SP, however, is mainly focused on the archaeology of (a) dehumanization and (b) educated transformation of the human condition. The problem of SW is, fundamentally, of legitimization and authenticity. Mere amalgamation of theory pluralism (Payne 2014; Turner 1996) does not make a theory of SW. Sheer organizational power and market values are poor substitutes for professional authenticity.[4]

---

[4] See my article 'Unification of Science, Knowledge and Truth', *International Journal of Contemporary Sociology.* Also, Mohan (2007).

Science, Social Sciences and Hope

In a chilling TV serial *Fortitude*, a mysteriously fictional drama unfolds where forces of perceived evil, actual science, public policy and local politics construct a futuristic reality in a remote paradise-like Norwegian island.[5] Of interest to us is the nexus of science and politics which shapes life and reality. The invention of atom bomb on the one hand and penicillin on the contrary significantly impacted the human condition. The hiatus between facts and values is a universal misfortune.

Critical social theorists, Habermas included, have 'recognized a distinctive relationship between "theory" and "practice"' (Keats 1981: 133; Mohan 2003).

Nearly half a century ago, John M. Romanyshyn edited a book for the CSWE (1974). The learned editor commissioned Ernest Becker to write a leading chapter on 'The discovery of the science of man' (Becker 1974: 7–32). This was a tailored but exceptionally brilliant and passionate essay to educate the scientists who have been focused on society as a subject. Based on his earlier masterpiece—and the most underrated yet one of the most erudite books ever written for working social scientists—Becker unravelled *The Structure of Evil* as 'an essay on the unification of science of man' (1968). I have seldom seen a reference to this book in a SW text. Archaeologically, I find the following excerpt, crucially relevant:

> The science of man, then, was gradually abandoned in favor of *scientists of man*.... The science of man was a passionate problem put forth by committed and hopeful men. It was the big discovery of the Enlightenment, incubating to its full size in the post-revolutionary

---

[5] '*Fortitude* is a British sci-fi psychological thriller television series created and written by Simon Donald. A 12-episode series was commissioned by Sky Atlantic in 2013, and started airing on 29 January 2015. The series is set in the fictional Arctic Norwegian settlement of Fortitude. On 9 April 2015, Sky Atlantic recommissioned the show for a second series consisting of 10 episodes, which premiered on 26 January 2017'. https://en.wikipedia.org/wiki/Fortitude_ (TV_series) (accessed on 4 October 2017).

world. It had to be approached cautiously and reverently, but it had to be plied into service for man—for man in society—for mankind as a whole. (Becker 1974: 10)

Services for people largely emerged in the post-War era subsequently reinforced by its ravages, fear in a viviparous world crowded by ideological–commercial–territorial domains. Social services evolved as a response to the anxieties triggered by the ghosts of an egalitarian philosophy that called for universal rights, equality and justice for all. However, to pre-empt any change in the industrial–military–corporate complex, a counter-nexus of social welfare agencies emerged.

American social welfare system in general, consciously and subconsciously, has served as a vehicle of counter-revolutionary force. This is an irony of the *Enlightenment* ethos. The *professionalized* SW is thus a tool of post-industrial society that thrives on its therapeutic impulses controlling, disciplining and punishing the people it seeks to *serve*. Masquerading in a myriad of venerated attires, equipped with diplomas and licenses, these practitioners basically thrive on their 'client's' helplessness. An elephant became a subject of specialized inquiry in a big social lab by a multitude of experts who studied the creature piece meal without understanding each other, defiling rather than healing the subject. Becker (1974) succinctly summed up the problem of human behaviour that scientists study from their own orientations without much comprehension of the whole reality. Becker writes:

Now, having reminded the disciplines of their central problems, a new and striking fact emerges—a fact which anyone reasonably conversant with the data of any one discipline cannot deny, namely, *that all the disciplines deal with aspects of one and the same question:* 'What makes people act the way they do?'—Interpersonally (social psychology), individually (psychology), in a society as a whole (sociology), between different societies (anthropology), and oddly in any society (psychiatry).' ... [No] discipline can answer the question satisfactorily, without knowing what all the other disciplines know about it. And the reason is, simply, that man lives in all these dimensions at the same time: individual, interpersonal, social, and social-deviant. (1974: 14 in Romanyshyn 1974)

It seems SW, though embedded in an interdisciplinary culture, has chosen to confine its approach to 'social-deviants' as a feckless attempt to justify itself in a therapeutic society.

Ethan Watters, in a thoughtfully provocative book *Crazy Like Us* (2010), writes:

> To travel internationally is to become increasingly unnerved by the way American culture pervades the world. ... We have the uneasy feeling that our influence over the rest of the world is coming at a great cost: loss of the world's diversity and complexity.... We are engaged in the grand project of Americanization.... (Watters 2010: 1)

Nothing is more globally contagious than 'the virus in us', writes Watters:

> There is no doubt that the Western mental health profession has had a remarkable global influence over the meaning and treatment of mental illness. Mental health professionals trained in the West, and in the United States in particular, create the official categories of mental diseases. The American Psychiatric Association's *Diagnostic and Statistical Manual of Mental Disorders,* the *DSM* (the 'bible' of the profession, as it is sometimes called), has become the worldwide standard. In addition, American researchers and organizations run the premier scholarly journals and host top conferences in the field of psychology and psychiatry. Western universities train the world's most influential clinicians and academics. Western drug companies dole out the funds for research and spend billions marketing medications for mental illnesses. Western-oriented traumatologists rush in wherever war or natural disasters strike to deliver 'psychological first aid', bringing with them their assumptions about how the mind becomes broken and how it is best healed. (2010: 3–4)

The new normal in SW is 'clinical'. From child welfare to 'military social work', curriculum designs to fieldwork, student evaluation to assignments and reviews, one cannot escape a perverse judgemental-ism that pervades the entire culture. One is perceived and treated as 'abnormal' unless certified by a 'supervisor' as acceptable. Once a colleague of Asian origin chided a racist white man in a disturbing faculty meeting. The furious authorities referred the Asian guy to the university's mental health centre where a 'licensed' psychologist diagnosed him as 'hypo-manic'.[6] An otherwise objective occupation conflicted by its contradictions has hypocritically become a judgmental vocation specialized in the politics of exclusion. I will publicly humiliate myself by letting the world know what it means to be marginalized in one's own home. A few examples are shared further.

It was not an easy task to develop a doctoral programme in a primarily vocational school. Since 2005, I could not teach a doctoral class, in the programme that I founded, because in the eyes of my successor/s I am neither a clinical researcher nor an empiricist. (In both cases, these unexplained, stupid characterizations were foolishly personal and patently racist.)

I have taught social policy my entire career. But now I am 'unqualified' to teach SW as I do not have a license to 'practise' from the Louisiana Social Work Education Licensing Board of Examiners. Practice? Yes, teaching is a 'practice'. Does it mean fieldwork supervisors, mostly fresh MSWs, should have PhDs and 300 research papers and books as essential credentials to qualify as 'teachers'? The application of multiple standards with impunity is SW's new strategy to censor and exclude people who seem 'different' ('deviant'?) or threatening to the DSM and 'licensed' congregations.

Bill Gates predicts the end of poverty by 2035. Bill and Melinda Gates, in their foundation's annual letter, debunk commonly held beliefs in development economics.[7] The richest man's view is almost diametrically opposed to the Holiest person on this planet. Nancy Gibbs sums up Pope Francis' view on capitalism:

> The Pope wants a Church that listens to the poor and values their contribution. He cautions against trickle-down economics and a 'crude and naïve' trust in the free-market of economic system,

---

[6] Circa 1986–1987.

[7] http://qz.com/169331/bill-gates-on-poverty-gmos-microsoft-and-vacationing-at-the-large-hadron-collider/ (accessed on 8 December 2017).

not as a matter of economic theory but because they too often let the powerful feed on the powerless and leave the poor without possibilities. (Gibbs 2013: 72).

Pope Francis challenged the US Congress to heal the open wounds of a bleeding civilization.[8]

When the age of anxiety morphs into the age of terror, the purpose of education ought to be re-examined in light of the philosophy of science and its evolution. We are 'waiting for datapocalypse', editorializes Andy Serwer (2014: 8). This new nihilism is deeply rooted in the archaeology of human behaviour. Psychiatric vigilantism is perhaps the worst form of 'help'. Social work licensing board/s indulge in this ugly strategy for less than ethical reasons. The colour of SWP in the United States is shrouded in cultural translucence and cognitive dissonance of various settings of practice. A secular–non-judgmental practice seems a logical impossibility.

Social Work as Its Own Nemesis

Under conditions of terror, most people will comply but some people will not. Humanly speaking, no more is required, and no more can reasonably be asked, for this planet to remain a place fit for human habitation.
—Hannah Arendt.[9]

'Fabrication of the Disciplinary Individual'[10] is Foucault's way of describing disciplinarity.

Dmitry Pisarev who influenced Russian social thought claimed that children and adolescents are great fanatics. Russian evolution is a beacon of revolutionary consciousness; Fabian socialism could

---

[8] http://www.nytimes.com/2015/09/25/us/pope-francis-congress-speech.html?_r=0 (accessed on 24 September 2015).

[9] Quoted by Roger Cohen in http://www.nytimes.com/2014/08/10/opinion/sunday/roger-cohen-the-gaza-war-and-israels-ethical-challenge.html?emc=edit_th_20140810&nl=todaysheadlines&nlid=42503955 (accessed on 10 August 2014).

[10] Expression borrowed from M. Foucault (1977[1995]): 308).

not reach its adulthood. Much of social intervention in the realm of social welfare is idealized with adolescent frenzy. SW as a profession exemplifies myopia of a self-serving theodicy without much existential relevance. SW's licensing boards tend to exercise questionable power beyond their authority. Even the Governor of Texas rescinded social work board's authority over university professors claiming that teaching is beyond their purview.

'Judgmentality' is ingrained in our repressive community's DNA. The developing world's schizophrenic attitude toward their Western colonizers is puzzling but understandable for a moment. Ernest Ugiagbe underscores the need for indigenization, a mantra that runs counter to universalization. Ugiagbe asserts 'to what extent indigenization of social work profession and practice in Nigeria can occur'.[11]

> There is a need to indigenize social work because of the shortcomings and inadequacies of Western social work theories and practices in addressing Nigerian social problems. For social work to succeed here, culture and tradition must be taken into consideration. Social work education and practices should incorporate some valuable local social–cultural practices. Social work should be indigenized in local contexts, that is, to accommodate the socio-cultural complexities of the over 350 ethnic groups and cultures in Nigeria. (Ugiagbe 2014)

From Africa to China to India to Latin America, one hears the contradictory messages between indigenization and internationalization, and between clientization and globalization. No wonder our identity crisis turns into paranoia when critically examined. Ironically, these concerns arise when the internationalists seek to westernize 'practice'. I question the morality and modality of those who *clientize* socio-economic miseries that are clearly attributable to the political vagaries of an irresponsible society. President Jimmy Carter's recent book is a call to action that challenges both world leaders and university

---

[11] http://isw.sagepub.com/content/early/2014/04/01/0020872813515013?papetoc (accessed on 9 May 2014).

chancellors and presidents to rethink about the purpose of education and SP (Carter 2014; also, Richard Pais 2012).

Talcott Parsons' structural–functional paradigmatic approach embodied American optimism to thwart post-War crisis and its impact on social structure, especially the middle class. Parsons' influence on sociology and social welfare still remains a dominant influence on post-industrial society and its policy which have shaped the organization and function of SW education. Alvin Gouldner sums it up:

> The empirical emptiness and abstractness of the Parsonsian analysis of order reflected an effort to respond to the international crisis that simultaneously threatened the middle class in capitalist countries on different levels of industrialization and with different political traditions. (1970: 145)

The dynamic social world has outlived Parsonsian theory. Even his definition of 'family' is no more valid. Global economy has changed the nature of capitalism. Socialism, the favourite bogyman of American scientists, has died.

The rise of utilitarianism, functionalism and positivism lent support to the state which seemed threatened by the forces of national and international changes. The residual safety net was nearly torn apart by depression and war. American pragmatism sought to 'pre-fix' the system before it stopped functioning. This was consciously in response to the threat that communism posed to substitute the ailing capitalist system. The invention of Welfare State was in fact a counter-revolutionary measure to offset the ominous dangers unleashed by radical transformation.

The New Deal was a systemic response to ward off such anxieties. Until the civil rights movements of the sixties and Johnson's war on poverty, the problems of the lower class did not actually emerge on the policy radars. Even in the twenty-first century, it is the ordeal of the middle class that matters. Nowhere have I seen a reference to the lower class; when 'underclass' was discovered in the early 1980s it produced a backlash against the Welfare State. Charles Murray became

Ronald Reagan's messiah of reform. Conservative punditry continues to fuel the anti-poor bigotry of public policy and practice.

Gary Becker, a student of Milton Freedman, won the Nobel Prize in 1992 'for broadening the horizons of economics, using economic analysis to explore social issues like crime, racial discrimination and drug addiction'. A giant in economics, Becker extended his theory of free market to marriage. In an NPR interview on the day he was awarded the Nobel Prize in economics, Becker explained:

> It's not an organized market the way the stock market is or a bazaar is in the Middle East, but it's a market nevertheless with the property that there are different people in this who are looking to get married. Not everybody can marry the same wonderful man or woman, and they have to make choices. And they may have met somebody who they're pretty happy with. They wonder about whether if they'd waited they'd meet somebody better, and these are the kinds of choices one makes in other markets. So, using market as a metaphor, but I think it's a very good metaphor for what goes on here.[12]

Becker, not unlike his guru Friedman, was a sceptic of government interference in markets, including redistribution of incomes to reduce rising inequality in the US. 'I think inequality in earnings has been mainly the good kind. I strongly believe it's been mainly the good kind', Becker said in 2007.[13]

If 'inequality is good', so is 'greed'. Remember Michel Douglas' character in *Wall Street*? No wonder why major economics Nobel Laureates have so miserably failed to solve any social problem of contemporary culture. If the queen of social sciences has a validity problem, its academic offspring's integrity cannot be taken seriously.

As Nietzsche would say, the origin always precedes the fall. Implicitly, we are reminded of our mandate: annihilation of poverty,

---

[12] http://www.npr.org/2014/05/05/309840501/remembering-economist-gary-becker-who-described-marriage-market (accessed on 5 May 2014).

[13] 'Remembering Economist Gary Becker, Who Described "Marriage Market"' by John Ydstie, National Public Radio, 5 May 2014, 4:02 PM ET.

inequality and injustice. No one remotely touches upon the archaeology of this oppression although 'diversity, oppression and social justice' are the sexiest slogan amongst the contemporary practitioners. Their entire pedagogy is narrowly focused on LGBT-related issues at the expense of true etiology of problems. As a consequence, a form of reaction-formation has perversely camouflaged the entire educational spectrum. Fetish, incomplete concepts play musical chair without signifying much. From strength perspective to attachment theory, evidence-based research to resilience theory, one finds bastardized concepts masquerading as new models. David Stoesz has a point: '[S]ocial work programs employ subjective, idiosyncratic indicators that do not permit comparisons across institutions or overtime' (2014: 385).

There was SP before SW came into practise. Gandhi's civil disobedience, Mandela's relentless protest against the violence of apartheid and King's historical equality march against racism and injustice are iconic exemplars of what SW professes to achieve. These giants were practitioners of hope, albeit unlicensed, without any MSWs and DSWs. Today Eveline M. Burns and Richard Titmuss are unqualified to teach social welfare policy in most of the schools of SW in the United States.

SW is, quintessentially, a soft vocational enterprise 'practised' as a *profession*. Its 'pioneers' embarked on a noble cause. However, its sub-terraria politics undermined its original mandate. Consequently, it continues to lack attributes of a profession: Its knowledge base is parasitic; its search for a uniquely autonomous identity is a delusion, and its effectiveness has always been in question. David Stoesz and Howard Karger et al. argue:

> From its inception in the late nineteenth century, social work has struggled to carry out the complex, sometimes contradictory, functions associated with reducing suffering, enhancing social order, and social reform.... *A Dream Deferred* chronicles this decline of social work, attributing it to the poor quality of professional education during the past half-century. The incongruity between social work's promise and its performance warrants a critical review of professional education. For the past half-century, the fortunes

of social work have been controlled by the Council of Social Work Education, which oversees accreditation of the nation's schools of social work.... Similarly, the quality of professional literature suffers from the weak scholarship of editors and referees. The caliber of deans and directors of social work educational programs is low and graduate students are ill-prepared to commence studies in social work. (2010; 2017)[14]

The authors primarily hold CSWE and organizational infrastructure responsible for poor quality of education. As I argued once, CSWE is us.

SW's relevance and legitimacy have not been self-evident. As a fulcrum of inanity and self-righteousness—a dangerous pretention—it has assumed a chameleon character that fits all occupational surroundings in quest of both survival and identity. The outcome is its eventual, unstoppable devolution. Numerical ascendance of its member schools, departments, students and practitioners does not testify to its authenticity. CSWE's perpetual thrusts to change its educational standards, organization and governance—put mildly—is a persistent proclivity to maintain mediocrity, power and status quo. *Journal of Social Work Education* editorializes:

> Other more pointed critiques, however, have involved blatant charges of mediocrity in our educational standards and professional culture, organizational hegemony coupled with self-serving elitism in our leadership, a monopolistic organizational stranglehold on accreditation standards, a total lack of accountability, ideological confusion, an overbearing ideology that thwarts academic rigor and independent scholarship, and even a call for only established scholars to serve on the COA (e.g., Markward & Drolen, 1999; Mohan, 2009; Stoesz & Karger, 2009). (Robbins 2014)

Sadly, as offered and practised, SW has become its own nemesis. Its contemporary thrusts are largely underwritten by private and public

---

[14] Cited from https://www.amazon.com/Dream-Deferred-Social-Work-Education/dp/0202363805/ref=sr_1_2?s=books&ie=UTF8&qid=1507406442&sr=1-2&keywords=Karger%27s+book+Dreams (accessed on 7 October 2017).

funds, including self-serving grants that maintain parochial interests. Academic institutions of higher education sustain it as a low-cost enterprise without according it a first-class citizenship. Its leadership in general is fashioned by political and marketplace considerations rather than sound academic credentials. The entire nomination, screening, selection, hiring and retention process is fraught with individual and group interests rather than institutional–professional goals.

Social work and psychoanalysis confront problems of theory testing. Karl Popper, comparing Freudian psychoanalysis, Marxism and Adlerian psychology with Einstein's theory of relativity proposed, 'falsifiability as the demarcation criterion between science and non-science; if a theory is untestable, unfalsifiable, it's unscientific' (Keats 1981: 135). SW's problem has fundamentally been aesthetico-archaeological. What does 'social' mean in real problem-solving? What does 'work' imply in professional practice? Sociological imagination, apparently in short supply, calls for appropriate self-identification and proper goal-orientation. The disconnection is emblematic of a split personality.

A full account of indignities, humiliation and discrimination that I suffered during my post-dean years spanning over quarter of a century (1986–2009) has impelled me to write a memoir, *Kafka's Cave* (Mohan 2018). I delayed this monograph to formulate a *theoria* regarding labyrinths of structural control. University as a system works rather impersonally with the exception of elitists' interests. Departmentally, it is a dog–eat–dog world where dogs and bitches wage a mutually destructive war. Marginalized people often suffer at the hands of those who claim entitlements and privileged benefits based on race, gender, sexual orientation and class. It is a tragedy how professionals play out this ultimately self-defeating game at the expense of discipline they profess to serve with hypocritical commitments, counterproductive licenses and inane codes. After 30 years of post-dean exclusion, I came to realize the basic inhumanity of 'social' in an otherwise noble calling. It is troubling to see the inhumanity of a benign creed in a toxic social environment.

'We are living', Bernie Sanders, told the Liberty University students,

> in a nation and in a world which worships not love of brothers and sisters, not love of the poor and the sick, but worships the acquisition of money and great wealth. I do not believe that is the country we should be living in. (*Time* 2015, September 28: 35)

Do you recall the last few words of Guru Dutt's immortal *Pyaasa*? Within my humble limitations, I have tried to achieve that civility. That is what led me to become a social worker.

Nietzsche's search for a *theoria* made him attempt to improve the human condition. He 'railed against charity, compassion and altruism in all their guises, whether Christian or otherwise' (Ferry 2003: 168). Nietzschean ethics involves an ontological *grand style* and *will to power*, that is, 'the will to will' which means maximum intensity of life to be lived to the full. He replaces *theoria* with genealogy, a tissue of forces of life involving chaotic, contradictory 'reactive' (negative) and 'active' drives and instincts. For a genealogist or deconstructivist, all 'objective' value judgments—because the value of life cannot be assessed—are foolish.

As of today, I have not come many social work educators who appreciate the ethos of this *theoria*. And I do not blame them. We are all products of our culture—a professional culture that has thrived on social romanticism at best. Much of DSM approach to human behaviour, which regulates mental health and social welfare industries, is based on subjective value judgments. Manifestations of poverty and social injustice are labelled in different judgemental inks that our 'practitioners' blame on varied human deficits and tragedies seldom caused by the victims of systemic oppression.

'Client–Practitioner' relationship is a hierarchized dyad of power and powerlessness. The Hippocratic Oath that has guided medical practice for ages becomes a joke when patients and their miseries are used for the practitioners' profit and greed. It is not difficult to understand why Howard Karger and David Stoesz have published such a devastating book on the performance of this august body (Carrillo, Karger, and Stoesz 2010).

A therapeutic society by definition is a sick, if not insane, society. *Clientization* is an admission of society's failures to come to terms with its own contradictions. A good society empowers its oppressed people rather than blames them for their misfortunes—poverty, cultural deficits and physical–mental incapacities. Much of modern 'practice' with clients is designed to follow these mantras of 'help'. The shamans of primitive medicine had no 'clients'; perhaps no slaves either. But they did *help* as the history of psychiatry reveals (Mohan 1973).

SW's evolution from raw sympathy delivered through a myriad of charities to professional 'practice' is devoid of empathy and authenticity. As a 'helping profession', it has assumed a godly status without any commitment for the resolution of causes of social–personal miseries. A professional obsession with evidence-based practice betrays a sense of humanity and reason. Its pretentious 'scientificity' is both farcical and misleading. A thorough content analysis of what we offer to students in the whole educational continuum would reveal a vocational orientation delivered in classroom and fieldwork settings, the basis for professionalized service. Now that online programmes are flourishing, its 'professional' status looks questionable. What is amply clear is that diplomas and licenses for 'practice' are tools of commoditization and institutionalism which regulate the powerless.

Careerism does not suit the ethical code of service professions, which includes medicine, law and SW. In our feverish bid to 'professionalize' our professional organizations—NASW and CSWE—have zealously mimicked both law and medicine to develop career tracks with ill-suited preparation and ill-equipped methodologies. Nowhere is this paradox more brazenly clear than in practice and research curriculums, not that other areas—human behaviour, social policy and fieldwork—are any less problematic. Susan Martin Robbins' editorial unravels conundrum of our curriculum and accreditation processes (2014).

Shoddy research is not a figment of critics' imagination. I have evaluated and have been evaluated by people whose conception of research is either sophomoric or scientifically stupid. Campus cronyism perpetuates the myths of a certain class of researchers who are either grants runners or locally powerful. University administrators support these 'research centres' because they bring money in terms of institutional support without much investment. I have never come across a SWR centre whose reports or findings have made any impact on the quality of education let alone the people whom they seem to serve. The mendacity of research practices in universities is scandalous if a true inventory of imposters is compiled. Forensic academics may one day become a necessary evil.

The establishment of Metaphysicians at Stanford University (*The Economist* 2014, March 15: 74) is indicative of the growth of 'sloppy' research. 'Why most research findings are false?' This is a question that a new discipline, meta-research, the *METRICS* system as called by Dr John Ioannidis, will answer (2014). If this is the state of the art in quantifiable, empirical, medical research, then all 'social research' seems to be an oxymoron at best, academic fraud at worst. In SW, research has not advanced from a primary level of development. A perusal of books and journals reveals at a glance how practitioners and educators camouflage their methodologies, themes and findings in overly co-authored reports.

SW's contemporary pedagogy is fundamentally anti-intellectual. Supervisory idolatry has marked the death of dissent in a supposedly liberating field. The outcomes are hardly anywhere close to authentic discoveries and findings that might be of any use in a cognate discipline. How many SW theorists and researchers are accepted and recognized in other social sciences? In a recent film *A Most Wanted Man*, Phillip Hoffman's character mocks a human-rights advocate by saying: 'You f___ing social worker protecting a terrorist!'.

Foucault, Parsons and Gouldner and Moynihan's Scissors

Moynihan's scissors is a phrase that has escaped no social scientist, especially those who find race—not racism—as a cause of persisting poverty. Conservative columnist George Will, whom I respect without always agreeing with his take on social issues, contends:

> In the 1960s, as the civil rights movement dismantled barriers to opportunity, there began a social regression driven by the explosive growth of the number of children in single-parent families. This meant a continually renewed cohort of adolescent males from homes without fathers; this produced turbulent neighborhoods and schools where the task of maintaining discipline eclipsed that of instruction. In the mid-1960s, Moynihan noted something ominous that came to be called 'Moynihan's scissors'....
>
> The assumption that the condition of the poor must improve as macroeconomic conditions, which the government thinks it can manipulate, improve is refuted by the importance of family structure. To say that poverty can be self-perpetuating is not to say...that poverty is caused by irremediable attributes that are finally the fault of the poor. It is, however, to define the challenge, which is to acculturate those unacquainted with the culture of work to the disciplines and satisfactions of this culture. (Will 2014: 7B)

Much of social science debate and public and social policy practice has been preoccupied with a spurious notion that has produced two ideologically apart dogmas: *culture* of *poverty* on the right and *blaming the victim* on the left. The outcome is that Reaganism, endorsed by social scientists such as Charles Murray, demonized the poor, which the leftists found as *blaming the victim*. As a consequence of this snake-and-mongoose tautology, poverty, its causes and remedies practically remain untouched, or neglected, by all policy interventions. Else, one would not witness a disturbing rise of inequality despite growth, government and globalization. *Governmentalism*,[15] however, prevails over the entire spectrum of policy–practice paradigm. *Super Crunchers* (Ayers 2007) can enhance productivity, governmental regulations, corporate profits and organizational effectiveness. The more they succeed the less they reduce inequality and injustice. This is the new law of economic Darwinism.

---

[15] A notion premised on Foucault's concept of 'governmentality'.

It is not the *culture of poverty*, it is the *poverty of culture* that blinds us (Mohan 2011). When I seek a paradigm shift in this ideologically combustive climate, *poverty of culture* becomes a fulcrum of new perspective that calls for transformational policy-action relative to the preventive and causative factors rather than dealing with symptomatic attributes: single-parent family, out-of-wedlock births, teenage motherhood and black poverty. The so-called 'Moynihan's scissors'[16] represents James Q. Wilson's sociological bias than imagination. The 'tangle of pathology' was equally an invention of a white intellectual elite who had neither experience nor vision to understand the cruel legacy of slavery (Coates 2017). It is breakdown of social institutions in general, not black family in particular, that has been at the core of Western decadence. Military, Church, University, Wall Street and family are all broken mirrors of a romantic fallacy.[17]

Since the objective of philanthropic charity was always guilt-ridden control, 'the carceral archipelago transported this technique from the penal institutions to the entire society' (Foucault 1977[1995]: 298). Foucault refers to 'technicians of behavior, engineers of conduct, orthopedists of individuality' who supervised, trained and disciplined in a gamut of hierarchized units with several results. One of the consequences that finally evolved into our contemporary SW is worth a note here:

> The second process is the growth of the disciplinary networks, the multiplication of their exchanges with the penal apparatus, the ever more important powers that are given them, the ever more massive transference to them of judicial functions; now, as medicine, psychology, education, public assistance, 'social work' assume an ever greater share of the powers of supervision and assessment, the penal will be able, in turn, to become medicalized, psychologized, educationalized, and by the same token that turning-point represented by the prison becomes less useful when, through the gap between its penitentiary discourse and its effect of consolidating

---

[16] http://www.pbs.org/fmc/timeline/ddisruption.htm (accessed on 24 March 2014); http://en.wikipedia.org/wiki/The_Negro_Family:_The_Case_For_National_Action (accessed on 24 March 2014).

[17] See, 'Man, and his madness', and 'A tale of two books'. http://www.sciaeon.org/sociology-insights/articles-in-press (accessed 6 March 2018).

delinquency, it articulates the penal power and the disciplinary power. (Foucault [1977]1995: 306)

We are all creatures of our culture. We adapt to its changing patterns and in turn transform its power-yielding mechanisms. Novelist Philip Roth, in his interview with Svenska Dagbladet published in *The New York Times*, said:

> The power in any society is with those who get to impose the fantasy.... Now the fantasy that prevails is the all-consuming, voraciously consumed popular culture, seemingly spawned by, of all things, freedom. The young especially live according to beliefs that are thought up for them by the society's most unthinking people and by the businesses least impeded by innocent end. (Roth 2014)

When *better angels of human nature* morph into *unfaithful angels*, society must revisit its contract with people. Freedom is not a unilateral subjective privilege; it is also a commitment to responsibility. Gatekeepers of society—policymakers, institutional heads, professionals including teachers and social workers—must guard against goals that have less than 'innocent ends'. A few important evaluative observations are submitted further for critical reflection:

Social welfare and social work settings are instrumentalities in functional apparatuses of a supervisory machine that modifies and controls people with social, economic and political deficits seemingly threatening to the established normative–punitive order.

The entire organization of SW education and practice zealously regulated by the profession's own elected and appointed elites in CSWE and NASW constitute a well-equipped 'perpetual-motion machine' (Gouldner 1970: 353) that regulates a conflicted world without much understanding of its inherent contradictions in an effort to educationalize coherence in a complexly diverse world.

SW's 'legitimacy' and existential rationale rests on its required hours of fieldwork (practicum or internship) modelled after law and medicine. Supervision, treatment, assessment and termination in private and public social agencies, including medical, psychiatric and correctional institutions are conducted by qualified 'supervisors' in liaison with faculty members in accredited schools and departments in educational settings. If the whole process is critically examined, one cannot escape the conclusion that students' learning experiences are panoptically monitored. This ensures faculty dominance and student acquiescence. This is rather an aberration of the profession's avowed goal: Achieving equality and justice without any real commitment to its accomplishment. Parsonsian social system is premised on 'equilibrium' rather than transformative change. It is no accident that SW's entire philosophical basis is organized around Parsons' mythology of system's immortality which unwittingly postulates karma and dharma.

The statements of unifying themes vary so wildly that it is hard to identify basic strands though each educational programme apparently goes through an accreditation process which is so loosely regulated but strictly governed for programme renewal and reaffirmation.

Knowledge base—episteme—is a crucial attribute of any profession. All mission statements aside, the rubber of reality hardly ever hits the road. SW's knowledge-based foundation is shaky at best; it is a myth generated by textbook writers who recycle borrowed constructs; they market fancy covers at the expense of students and their families.

National and international boundaries have abstractly collapsed in a new world order transformed by information revolution, globalization and free market economies. Obsolescence of social science offers no pathways to liberate the oppressed ones. Yet American SW continues to be the model followed by most developing nations.

Internationalization of social problems has changed the colour and magnitude of problems that traditionally belonged to the Welfare State. Since the 'State' itself is under attack by new libertarians and various terrorist organizations, refugees, destitute, homeless and the poor are nobody's concern. Look what is happening in Europe after the collapse of civil society in Syria. Implications of this situation are horrifying. While social services and their professionals could alleviate some suffering, the policy and practice structures are dated and dysfunctional.

Since 'thinking-by-numbers is the new way to be smart' (Ayers 2007), social scientist's evidence-based practice and research will be dominated by *Super Crunchers* whose brave new world—of equation verses expertise—reduces all decision-making to statistical determinism. This amounts to near dissolution of reflective, intuitive and discursive practices that have been the hallmark of 'sociological imagination'. SW's new wave of web-based, profit-making, internet-driven MSW diplomas will not—and cannot—achieve its primordial quality of practice. Mere quantification and efficiency do not improve quality and effectiveness. Above all, the nature of scientism changed after 9/11/2001. Sure, paranoid too have their enemies but savants and sages need not be schizophrenic fools.

The aforementioned observations, if seen within the following theoretico-archaeological context, will validate my long-time assertion that American SW—like sociology—fundamentally adheres to the Parsonsian gospel that maintains the system rather than transforms it:

> Rather than focus on change, Parsons' analysis of social systems long tended to emphasize that they are governed by self-maintaining processes and to highlight the *order*-maintaining mechanism inherent in them. Along with this, he had a pronounced and one-sided tendency to conceive of conformity—with the expectations of others and with the requirements of moral codes—as conducive to the stability of social systems. The Parsonsian 'social system' is a social world with its own ramifying network of defenses against tension, disorder, and conflict: pierce one, and another springs up, ready to cushion shock. The system's stability may be contingent, but it is never precarious. What is stressed is its almost endless capacity to absorb and nullify shock; what is painstakingly displayed is an intricate and interlocking network of mechanisms that binds the system's energy into itself, and swiftly and efficiently distributes it to stress-points, and never dissipate any of it. (Gouldner 1970: 352)

Gouldner's summation is an apt characterization of SW's own strength and weakness. Strength perspective's denial of its weaknesses and evidence-based practice's blindness to the realities of life is a shocking commentary. The utter failure leadership sustains a rotten system. Propotonics of higher education constitute of a hierarchized bureaucracy of hideous trappings masquerading as society's 'gate-keepers'.

A closer study of history reveals that revolutions preceded dictatorial tyrannies from Paris to Peking. The rise of social development marks the evolution of welfare consciousness. Developmentalism became a reality when Harry Truman first spoke about the 'developing' nations. In the post-World War era, Western democracies rethought of the decolonized regions, the Third World, and began dispensing advisory and material support for political reasons. This has brought changes in the institutional structure of the postcolonial world but cultural transformation has never been achieved. The duality of India's paradoxical success and failure is a case in point. The same could be said of Indian SW.

A decolonized traditional society masquerading as democracy has to offer much more than an illusion of progress. So far, India has failed to provide its teeming millions a sense of security and a safety net of social–economic protection despite its avowed democratic ideals and professed policy directions. In the absence of a socially committed political structure, its fractured politics and predatory culture has left a billion people in search of dream that still romanticizes the brutish colonial rule. Serendipitously, an educated, consumerist English-speaking middle class serves the ends of a post-feudal society that worships personality cults, identity entitlements, morally bankrupt government and a failed educational–military–establishment that thrives on developmental delusions. A sea change in South Asia is an inescapable reality. Basic quality of life, decency and security still remain a distant dream.

Transformational Challenges

'Trying to understand love is like trying to understand the weather—complex, but essentially full of the kinds of patterns that mathematics can interpret', says John Gottman, 'the Einstein of love' (Ohlson 2015: 77).

As the preceding analysis reveals, both altruism (individual) and welfare (social) belong to the same spectrum. But the children of Charles C. Darwin cannot see his revenant. SW's devolution is an outcome of this dissonance.

Commoditization of basic needs—education, health and social solidarity—may have enriched certain sectors of economy and populace but it has hopelessly changed the contours of life. The tranquillizing impact of mythology and fantasy helps people who cannot buy quality education, required health care and necessities of life.

SW confronts three main challenges which include deal with (a) cultural conundrums of the new elites and their pseudo-modernity, (b) salience of appropriate modalities of action and (c) corruption in higher education that has feverishly privatized moneymaking, vocational programmes without much congruence with reality. India's poor, underprivileged, tribal and displaced people pose a terrifying spectacle while corporate businesses bloom and political elites live rapaciously.

Lack of what Brené Brown calls 'self-consciousness' (2015) is one of social work's misfortunes. Aping a failed model is counterproductive. Again, it is one thing to market 'shame' as a 'self-help' guide that sustains a therapeutic industry; it is a daunting challenge to swim against the current of counter-development. SW has become a mirror; it is not a flame. Our moon reflects borrowed light; it does not generate energy. This planet ravaged by the scourges of poverty, inequality, war and terror needs synergy of transformative disciplines.

A few non-social work leaders have delivered amazing results in uplifting poor and exploited children. Some NGOs are equally involved in social action and mental health. Professional organizations should lend support to voluntary public service without envying their accomplishments. There is no society without social problems. It bodes well for professional careers but it mocks at dysfunctional democracies that pride themselves as a global force.

HSD calls for unification of knowledge, technology and productivity. Academic and professional disciplines that failed to achieve the Enlightenment goal are destined to devolve. The mimic profession is ill-equipped at best to achieving this stupendous goal. Its 'otherness' is a self-created necessity of self-alienation.

As work will cease to exist in the emerging patricidal-acquisitive mendaciously new consumerist culture, SW will become a victim of its own success. Since our guilt is misplaced, we need to learn from failures. Acceptance of one's shortcomings is a better rationale for 'strength perspective'. Recognition of failure, rather than gloss of phony success, is the crux of self-renewal. A hedonist, hubristic culture breeds institutional narcissism. To reinvent post-Enlightenment consciousness, it is prudent that we synergize the imperatives of *Enlightenment Two*[18] (Mohan 2011, 2015b).[19]

[18] Enlightenment consciousness is regaining recognition. See *Enlightenment Now* (Pinker 2018).

[19] I am profoundly grateful to the Indian Social Work Congress 2015 and the NAPSWI for their invite to give a keynote address titled 'Community Engagement, Social Responsibility, and Social Work Profession' at the Jain Vishwa Bharti Institute, Ladnun under the inspiring leadership of my esteemed colleague Professor (Dr) R.B.S. Verma, Professor and Head, VBI, Rajasthan, India. It was my distinct privilege to address certain issues that I consider crucial for HSD and corresponding social policies, programmes and programmes as unified components of what I call social practice. I am doubly fortunate to avail of this unique opportunity to submit this monographic keynote in honour of a living legend, Dr S. Zafar Hasan, my teacher, friend, philosopher and mentor. I am solely responsible for the imperfections of this document.

Seven Pillars of Social Practice

> If extinction is a morbid topic, mass extinction is, well, massively so.
>   —Elizabeth Kolbert (2015: 3).

This chapter, 'Seven Pillars of Social Practice', represents the ethos and substance of *unification* (Mohan 1999). It signifies SW as a flame rather mirror. A brief structure and essential elements of this approach are spelled out in the sections that follow.

All 'work' is social. Social scientists, hopefully, will not subject the *social* to the dogmas of unprincipled scrutiny. The micro–macro dualities despite the dominance the 'clinical', continue to balkanize epistemologies of change. SP is conceptualized as an imminent outcome of SW, an evolution rather than refutation.

SW's *status quoism* and habitual chameleon nature has cost its identity. It is sadly unrecognized in the centres of power since a dissonance of the establishmentarians impede clearer reasoning. SP is reflective, transformative action; as a calling, it may transcend SW's inherent limitations. SP's nature and scope is envisioned as universal with full awareness of human banalities. SW's stereotypical roles do not limit SP's approach. Sarvepalli Radhakrishnan sums it up:

'The human being is a *samsarin*, a perpetual wanderer, a tramp on the road' (Schilpp 1952: 47). But I had my epiphany when I read Kabir in 1952, the year I flunked in 8th grade:

Pothi padh padh jag mua, pundit bhayo na koy
Dhaai akhar prem ke, jo padhe so pandit hoy.[1]

Kabir was a fakir, poet, philosopher and unschooled illiterate who transformed South Asian culture. Today he may be executed for blasphemy in the dark alleys of extremist regimes. I read him in junior high school and it changed my life forever (Mohan 2018).

A SW professor named Brené Brown gets *Time's* recognition for her bestselling *Gifts of Imperfection* (2015). She says: 'Guilt, embossment, humiliation and shame: they're the emotions of self-consciousness' (*Time* 2015, September 21: 88).

'Shame is a revolutionary sentiment', Karl Marx wrote famously. Nietzsche's dictum—something that does not kill you, will make you stronger—has been totemic guide. The barriers that a child outlives in rural India and comes all the way to the United States with US $8.00 knows what failures exist under the glass ceilings of an advanced culture (Mohan 2018).

Seven Algorithms to Practice

'Science is a way of thinking much more than it is a body of knowl-edge', Carl Sagan famously said. Human beings make errors. To err is human. But to kill 5,000 people in a weekend traffic is insanity. That is why, we will have self-driven cars. In a dazzlingly brilliant book *Algorithms to Live By*, two scientists untangle some human dilemmas:

There is a particular set of problems that all people face, problems that are a direct result of the fact that our lives are carried out in

---

[1] 'Reading books where everyone died, none became anymore wise/One who read the world of "love" only becomes wise' (Trans. by author).

finite space and time.... They might seem like problems unique to human; they're not. Talking about algorithms for human lives might seem like an odd juxtaposition.... Long before algorithms were ever used by machines, they were used by people.... Algorithms have been a part of human technology ever since the Stone Age. (Christian and Griffith 2016: 2–4)

SP, like algorithms, still does not have a natural disciplinary home. SP is postulated as a fulcrum of seven pillars of professional ethics, skills, values and wisdom. Its main planks deal with the ontology and politics of an otherwise noble profession. The professional trajectory of SW evolves from primitive altruism subsequently enforced by organized philanthropies to 'help' people on the fringes of communal cohesion. Various systems of faith institutionalized helping modalities that offered subsistence for survival without ever attacking at the roots of societal evils. Academic SW today is guided by organizational necessities rather than principles.

The unintended consequences of war brought the Welfare State as a buffer to offset the fears of communism. The (Parsonsian) American Welfare system, as Alvin Gouldner has vividly argued in *Coming Crisis of Western Sociology* (1980), was meant to be a capitalist barrier to the rising spectre of communism. In the post-American century, we have witnessed not only the meltdown of statist dogmas but also the State itself. Thanks to Bernie Sanders, 'socialism' is no more a dirty word in American politics.

Innate human proclivities call for deeper analysis. Change is uncertain but normally good; transformation is better. The banality of life's human conditions impels us to rethink about the genesis of social problems and our world view towards a better future.

The structure sketched out further is a formative–conjectural framework to redesign SW education and practice. Its seven dimensions clearly delineate the relevant aspects of SP as a valid academic discipline.

Mission, Education and Service

Mission

Purpose and goal of SP as an academic discipline has to be redefined; its centrality to institutional objectives is crucial. This may be a call for revisiting the crisis of higher education.

Education

SP's continuum does not encourage doctoral level (much of SW research tends to be ill-advised, duplicitous or pretentious; interdisciplinary knowledge base is encouraged without necessarily emphasizing doctoral research; education implies instruction, fieldwork, research and inquiry in field, policy and practice areas; SP does not employ 'client–practitioner' dyad as a model; *clientization* is essentially a repressive, anti-dialogical practice; SP's approach employs friendly, cathartic situations. In other words, integrate research and knowledge with life-saving skills in dialectically holistic, didactic pedagogies of change.

Service

SP's realm of service is inclusive of public and private sectors that might benefit from professional advocacy, liaison and non-profit networks of change; guided 'service' is an excellent ground for teaching, learning, research and self-renewal.[2]

---

[2] Much of SWR is service. 'When I worked in child protection, I never had the kind of opportunities for research I see in the NHS. Social work is missing a trick', notes Rachel Sempija.

'Researcher-practitioners are less common in social work than other helping professions, such as clinical psychology'. While the need for a research culture is well taken, it is basically an emphasis on what is popularly called evidence-based practice. http://www.communitycare.co.uk/2017/07/24/social-workers-need-research-culture/ (accessed on 30 July 2017).

There is a symbiotic relationship in the three elemental sectors of mission, education and service (MES). The simplicity of this model underscores its universality and relevance in a fast-changing globalized world.

Empathetic humility (EH): Empathy without humility is hypocrisy and arrogance; SP practitioners are not 'experts'; they are exemplars.

Liberatory assistance (LA): There is no room for 'help' which often involves patronizing relegating the recipient to a stigmatized status. LA refutes 'liberation by oppression'.

Transparent effectiveness (TE): While confidentiality is an essential aspect of all professional services, SP's emphasis is on transparent effectiveness which means public accountability of services rendered.

Buoyance finally undergirds all six elements as a metaphysical system.[3] Life's stressors and pressures can be confronted by buoyance and speed that keep one afloat during a perfect storm. This serves as a metaphor for SP's unified synthesis of MES and EH, and LA and TE.

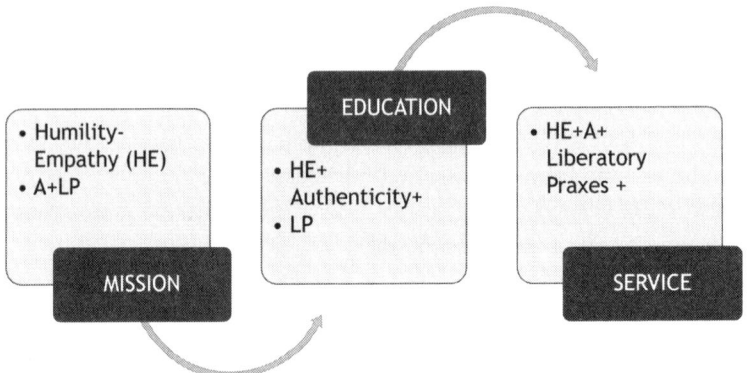

Figure 7.1 *The 7th Pillar of Social Practice*
(Buoyance + Speed Defying Gravity)

[3] I appreciated the significance of buoyance while taking swimming lessons from Johanna at South Side YMCA. Her physics of swimming includes buoyance with momentum (speed) as a way of life to remain afloat defying gravity, an invincible force.

The aforementioned seven pillars are tenets of a professional disciplinarity that seeks to use and develop knowledge in the service of human kind in congruence with the Enlightenment values.[4] The attributes, just listed, are not exhaustive; it is a work-in-progress as depicted further.

Ontology and Practice

The 'will' to practice is an inner force; it is emblematic of ethics to serve. The outcome is not a commodity; it is an impulse, a feeling unmatched by any quantifiable reward. At the end of each semester, I usually asked my MSW students to do something nice to a person without letting her/him know what you did. I found this mantra of service more rewarding than a formal recognition or reward. This is a seed of revolutionary consciousness which sprouts inside you to 'build your life and those of the people around you into a plateau of intensity that would have afterimages of its dynamism that could be reinjected into still other lives…. Deleuze and Guattari call it revolution' (2011: xv).

Civilization is both culmination and acculturation of work required to survive in the world. Work is non-libidinal; human 'aversion to work' is fount of discontent (Freud 1961: 34). The purpose of *practice* is sublimated joy in an otherwise unpleasant world. The dialectic of this approach is underscored by Freudo–Marxian ethics. Humans cannot go back to the primitive stage but they can minimize civilizational stressors. Freud's interpretation of the Prometheus myth is premised on the notion that repressed work is fundamental to civilizational growth. By implication, we live in a dangerous world. Ontology of varied relation to *being* is an existential reality facilitated by practices of hope.[5]

---

[4] There is no intent to emulate Deepak Chopra's *The Seven Spiritual Laws of Success*. Postmodern gurus of 'success' idolize founders of Facebook and Amazon as exemplars. Oscar Wilde was right: There is something vulgar about success.

[5] One of the pervasive social problems in India (and elsewhere) is bride-burning or dowry deaths. A simple solution to end this scourge is a realization:

Environmental justice (EJ) is preferred as a unifying theme to be elaborated in the next chapter. SW has used HBSE as a required component to emphasize coping and adaption in the life cycle. Think of a community in the 'cancer valley' of Louisiana. There is no escape from the poisonous injustices that are forced on helpless people. It is only the poor and marginalized people who live in the darkest alleys of industrial culture.

Ontology of a profession is built on the primordial structure of values and skills that evolve into a fulcrum of specialized body of scientific practice.

This is a philosophically grounded self-reflective investigation with findings that merit attention from academics, university administrators, researchers, public policymakers, SW students and practitioners. The American creed is betrayed by its own contradictions in practice. SW, which should have been the candle, has become a mirror of the social meltdowns that endanger the foundations of a civil society.

George Orwell, reflecting on M.K. Gandhi wrote: 'No doubt alcohol, tobacco, and so forth, are things that a saint must avoid; but sainthood is also a thing that human beings must avoid'. SW is the saint of social sciences. Yet, its practitioners are also called 'unfaithful angels'. This section offers a nexus of justice and freedom that unburdens humanity from the toxicity of its own trappings.

Altruism pre-existed civilization. There was no racism when humans lived in caves. There was benevolence before social welfare became a residual function. Social problems persist despite social work/welfare and policy. Disease, malnutrition and child abuse plague humanity in spite of advancements in medical and social sciences. This essay seeks to 'reset' a dated mindset; it is *the poverty of culture* (and imagination) that bedevils humanity (Mohan 2011). It sustains a predatory system of deprivation and violence.

Treat your daughter-in-law (DiL) as your own daughter. Your own daughter is a (would be) DiL. Once the ontology is brought to action, 'practice' becomes 'social'. You do not need to be a client of a licensed social worker to achieve this goal. This simple example is offered to signify the essence of SP.

Enhancing SW's effectiveness and relevance is the main purpose of SP. The objectives, specifically, deal with three dimensions and certain points of HSD. A symbiotic system of linkages welds theory and practice that promotes transformative knowledge. The theoretical basis of this unifying framework is largely owed to Freudo–Marxian–Nietzschean–Sartrean–Foucauldian–Gandhian philosophies in contrast with SW's populist vocational approaches akin to an archipelago of related but disconnected perspectives.[6]

SW's contemporary curricular designs involve certain required and specialized courses in a two-year sequence. HBSE, social welfare policy, research and SP constitute the foundation based on which a myriad of specializations deal with different fields from child welfare to mental health generally incorporating agency-based fieldwork under supervised settings. Coping, adaptation and counselling form a culture that a therapeutic society employs to 'clientize' the victims of a rapacious environment. Environmental justice, as contended earlier, underscores the dynamics of human conditions, which deal with both needs and behaviours.

Human alienation continues to be a mega problem that neither social sciences nor global democracies have been able to resolve. Contemporary SW's shortcuts to problem-solving are grounded in alternate reality.

If SW is based on flawed assumptions about HSD, what should we do about it? This is formidable question. This pivotal chapter has three strands. First, it builds a case for a new professional discipline based on liberatory praxis; second, SP might rise like a phoenix from the ashes of SW and, finally, illustration of the seven major pillars to legitimize SP. As a fulcrum of knowledge-based practice, it offers hands-on experiential knowledge, exemplars and suggestions relative to transformation of SW.

---

[6] There are two texts about SW theory (Turner 1996 and Payne 2005). They tend to relate various theories to SWP with or without much relevance. A jack of all trades gathers no moss. Interlocking is not 'unifying'.

I am troubled by the universities' recruitment policies and their cheap 'sales-pitches' to enroll young men and women in SW programmes. Social workers are one of the most underpaid professionals. Thanks to the law of functional market values.

'Today's gadgets are just the latest out-there attempts to relive pain, stress, and depression', says John Brandon (Leigh Buchanan 2015). Social workers, the 'clone troopers' of a therapeutic society, play a new Jedi who has morphed into an evil. The question is: How to reclaim lost innocence? Is it possible to go back to 65 generations?

Reclaiming lost 'innocence' (commonsense and sanity) in 'the age of unreason' (*The Economist* 2015, July 11) is mission impossible. 'As the world grows richer and older, mental illness is becoming more common'. John Prideaux considers the consequence (*The Economist* 2015, July 11). Global implications of mental illness are seldom discussed in any discourse. This is an issue Diagnostic and Statistical Manual of Mental Disorders (DSM -5) will never be able to address. It is my contention that we ought to revisit the nexus of both ontogenesis and phylogenies before launching any post-Welfare State programme of consequence.

Finally, SP is no panacea. Its trajectory involves elements of a journey towards a free and equal society without oppressive unfreedom that breed dehumanization. SP will transcend its vocational purpose morphing into a renewed force of intuitive self-empowerment.

'The math affords new insights interrelationships. For example, it reveals that the most resilient of all couples are conflict avoiders', asserts Gottman, the man who believes that Albert Einstein helped the Allied forces win the war. (Ohlson 2015: 76–81). Like human relationships, social interactions and processes—so far left to the realm of subjective–interpretative sciences—will radically transform into technologically advanced practices that leave little room to any soft profession. This transformation will require social practitioners to be a different breed of 'helpers', if they are willing to accept the challenges of time. History suggests that many a culture died due to its inability to evolve. What I call *Uberization of social services* is imminent as technology and conservatism advance globally and hand-in-hand.

Brad Stone's words about his formidable bestseller *The Upstarts* should be read seriously:

> It is instead a book about pivotal movement in the century-old emergence of a technological society. It's about a crucial era during which all regimes fell, new leaders merged, new social contracts were forged between strangers, the topography of cities changes, and the upstarts roamed the earth. (2017: 14)[7]

[7] As the subtitle of the book—*How Uber, Airbnb, and the Killer Companies of the New Silicon Valley Are Changing the World*—suggests, the field of social welfare cannot be left untouched in the wake of these tectonic social changes. Killer companies have however taken on some basic human needs of a growing society. Uber resolved transportation headaches; Airbnb has almost solved the problem of accommodation; likewise, social services will be resolved soon in the Post-Apple–Google–Facebook era by the entrepreneurial spirit lurking in the fog of welfare conundrums (Stone 2017).

CHAPTER 8

Environmental Justice: A Practice Model

At magic hour, when the sun has gone but the light has not, armies of flying foxes unhinge themselves from the Banyan trees in the old graveyard and drift across the city like smoke. When the bats leave, the crows come home. Not all the din of their homecoming fills the silence left by the sparrows that have gone missing, and the old white-backed vultures, custodians of the dead for more than a hundred million years, that have been wiped out. The vultures died of diclofenac poisoning.

—Arundhati Roy (2017: 5).

Social Justice and Environment

Man is by nature a social animal, an individual who is unsocial naturally and not accidentally, is either beneath our notice or more than human. Society is something in nature that precedes the individual. Anyone who either cannot lead the common life or is so self-sufficient as not to need to, and therefore does not partake of society, is either a beast or god.

—Aristotle, *Politics*, c.328 BC.

Theories of social justice have ignored, rather conveniently, the environmental imperative that defines and shapes the shades of justice in different culture.[1,2]

The Paris Agreement is the closest global consent on any issue that confronts humanity.[3] The conflict between economic growth and EJ partakes of myopic view which the United States has taken. In the context of this book, it speaks volumes how reason and science are easily sacrificed in policymaking. My notion of social psychology (SPsy) as a discipline underscores social practice as formulated in this book.

Social Psychology Practice, Science and Injustice

SP studies inequality in light of environmental injustices that impact human lives. 'New research indicates', *The Economist* writes, 'not only that climate change will impose heavy costs on the American economy but also that it will exacerbate inequality' (15 July 2017: 66). The following findings can hardly be overstated:

> The study shows that the pain of climate change will fall more heavily on America's poorest bits than its richest areas…. The rich are the disproportionate contributors to the carbon emissions.

[1] This chapter is based on my editorial Introduction to *Construction of Social Psychology* (Mohan 2015; 2016).

[2] The idea of 'environmental justice' dominated my thinking when I was commissioned to establish an international journal *Environment and Social Psychology* by Whioce Pub., Singapore (ISSN: 224-7979). The goal and objectives of this journal and forum fundamentally conceptualize rationale and parameters of environmental justice, which I believe is of paramount significance to achieving equality (Mohan 2016). Construction of social psychology (CSP) and environmental justice are almost symbiotically used in this chapter.

[3] https://www.nature.org/ourinitiatives/urgentissues/global-warming-climate-change/the-paris-agreement-what-does-it-mean.xml?src=sea.AWG.prpari.crv1&gclid=EAIaIQobChMIm4awh_Sz1QIVCo9pCh233wSYEAAYAiAAEgIubPD_BwE (accessed on 31 July 2017).

That power climate change. It is cruel and perverse, therefore, that the costs of warming should be disproportionately borne by the poor. And it is both insult and injury that the wealthy are more mobile in the face of climate-induced hardship, and more effective at limiting the mobility of others. The strain this injustice places on the social fabric might well lead to woes more than damaging than rising temperatures themselves. (*The Economist* 2017, July 15: 66)

Science, Sam Harris contends, 'should be considered a specialized branch of a larger effort to form true beliefs about events in our world' (2010: 195). Harris argues that values translate into facts that can be scientifically understood: 'moral truth can be understood in the context of science' (2010: 2). The 'moral landscape', therefore, involves human well-being within scientific discourse.

SPsy, a sociological offshoot of psychology, is conceptualized here as a disciplinarity that unravels the human experience in its varied dimensions involving conditions, interactions and behaviours at different levels of existence. 'Culture defines us within the context of neuroscience and psychology' (Harris 2010: 2).

Construction of social psychology (CSP) is in fact a reconstruction of the duality that forged professional alliances between intercognate disciplines. Exploration of human–social interaction and development posits SPsy as an independent field of study and research beyond Cartesian dualism and interdisciplinary hybridism. Society is an abstraction. I doubt if society preceded humans. Also, we must, at the very outset, question the Aristotelian premise that man is a 'social animal'. Perhaps, man is a political creature, socio-psychologically. From times immemorial, societies have developed around cultural norms that continue to regulate human behaviour. Each culture's world view offers a perspective on life. Human societies, both as abstractions and congregates, embody primordial philosophical paradigms that help the *construction* and *deconstruction* of SPsy.

While *psychology* got prefixed with *social* mainly in the post-War era of the twentieth century, new realities of the twenty-first century call for transformative reflection on the nature and scope of its subject.

My contention: A climate with numerous social–cultural meltdowns calls for redefinition of *social psychology*.

The factors that account for this new direction are related to: (a) inequality in a globalized culture; (b) anti-state counter-revolutions (ISIS, for example); (c) breakdown of social institutions that defined individual, family and marriage and community as bases of that formed the primordial basis of social contract that does not exist today.

It is a tragic irony that philosophy as a discipline is losing ground while techno–material specialties are riding the tide of success. These advancements, we contend, cannot liberate humanity from its innate trappings. In fact, there lurks an ominous threat for human survival. Artificial Intelligence (AI) and its future is a determinant force to reckon with.

The main objective of this chapter is to demystify *the power of materialism at the expense of philosophical streams* that undergird all SPs. We use continental philosophy as a base for the *deconstruction* of SPsy, an alternative scenario to save the world from itself. Implicit here is our a priori assumption that essentialist theories and practices have diminished humanity. The chapter will synthesize both the Western and Eastern philosophies to analyze this hypothetical formulation.

SP's construction calls for reexamination of the nexus of environment and human behaviour. This thrust is embedded in three basic connections: (a) sustainability and HSD, (b) interdisciplinarity of approaches and (c) paradigmatic perspective on a full behavioural spectrum. In other words, SP seeks to:

- Examine the possibilities of HSD as a credible paradigm for scientific inquiry and dialogue that promote world peace, prosperity and progress in a dangerously complex world.
- Transcend dualities and contradictions of contemporary ideologies and methods toward a unifying framework for enduring social psychological research.
- Promote scholarly pursuits for the advancement of knowledge in search of empirical evidence and truth, which support environmental justice as a viable paradigm conducive to HSD.

Unravel social psychological barriers—beliefs, attitudes, stereotypes, prejudices, habits and politico-cultural practices—that thwart quality education and learning beyond the contemporary dogmas of behavioural schools.

- Interface pathways to understand and resolve contemporary nihilism that incubates psychopathologies of self-destructive addictions—sexual abuse, substance and drugs, interpersonal murders and terror.[4]

The Age of Anxiety has morphed into the age of sudden terror. How did this social transmutation occur? What forces triggered this biosocial metamorphosis? Was it epigenetic or biogenetic? Can we scientifically ascertain the future of human race given the circumstances that are at work? It is my assumption that a paradigm shift is overdue to construct afresh a new way of studying science, humanities, social sciences in particular. In other words, *environmental justice* is posited as a fulcrum of new pathways to unrevealing attitudinal and behavioural manifestations relevant to SP. 'Of all branches of social psychology, none seems to have as much intuitive appeal as does social psychology' (Baron and Graziano 1991). Initially, fundamentals of SPsy are embedded in the interdisciplinary study of three intertwined aspects of 'humanology and technology' undergirding the interactional processes of (a) communication, (b) socialization and (c) individual in the group (Hartley and Hartley 1961). SPsy has thus traditionally dealt with interpersonal relationships in a societal context with emphasis on beliefs and attitudes, perceptions and realities that impact social functioning of people in a particular culture. Implicitly, social conflict, change, accommodation and cooperation are invisible and invincible forces that impact human behaviours and interactions. Therefore, no static, essentialist theory of social psychological process can be formulated.

CSP involves 'creative and critical processes' (McGuire 1999). William J. McGuire studied attitudes, persuasion and social influences

---

[4] *Environment and Social Psychology*, published by Whioce Publishing, Singapore, December 2015. http://esp.whioce.com/index.php/ESP/index (accessed on 1 June 2015).

that undergird his learning theory underlying ephemeral aspects of human thoughts, behaviours and actions encompassing the whole spectrum of critical processes. He sought to study:

> the magical experiments on attitude inoculation showing that small doses of a persuasive message can increase resistance to later larger doses; the construction of self in terms of its distinctive and atypical features; the content, structure, and processing of thought system functioning by balancing logical consistency, realistic coping, and hedonic gratification; persuasion by Socratic questioning that selectively directs attention; and the process of doing research as an exciting and infinitely rewarding activity. (1999: cover)

The 'social problem approach to scientific SPsy involving individual, interpersonal and group processes' (Baron and Graziano 1991) seems to signify SP's role from a logical and pragmatic viewpoint. Symbolic interactionism along with internalization and differentiation, socialization, power and deviance has added depth and authenticity to comprehend and resolve complicated aspects of SPsy (Denzin, Lindesmith, and Straus 1975; Backman and Secord 1966).

In the last seven or eight decades, human ingenuity has brought an order in a rather chaotic world. One could also against this premise. Nonetheless, it cannot be gainsaid that human experiences and innovations have metamorphosed social reality. There is a three-dimensional paradox of this emerging phenomenon which, I contend, should be the new focus of all SP research:

Figure 8.1 seeks to interface three intertwined (A, B, C) bases of bio–social–personal foundations of an interactional sphere where roots of human behaviour lay grounded relative to (a) ... (b) ... and (c) .... The womb of this bio-interactional design of HSD is embedded in the sociocultural whole that shapes, modifies and manipulates the raw trappings of one's intrapsychic world. The major streams of psychological and sociological thought broadly underscore the unification of SP as illustrated in Figure 8.1.

Instinctual, institutional and intellectual—rational and irrational—motives and impulses are embedded in evolutionary and developmental

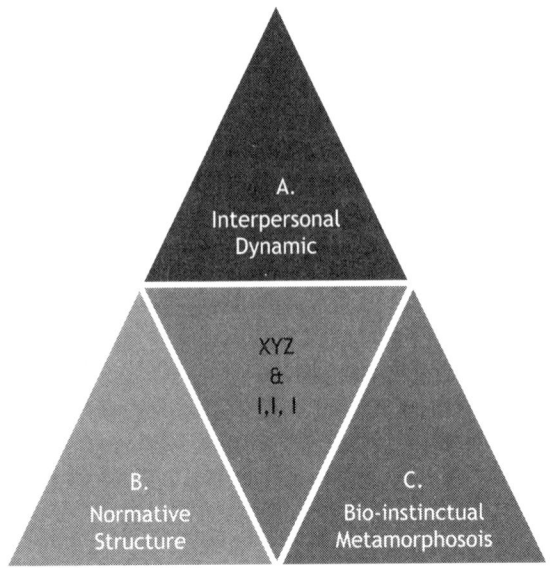

A = Interpersonal Dynamic (ID)
B = Normative Structure (NS)
C = Bio-instinctual Metamorphosis (BIM)

Frontiers of a discipline: SPsy
Contexts: Social, cultural, political and economic
Development and techno-digital Revolution

Figure 8.1 *Emergence of a Discipline: A Framework*

phases of human experience. SPsy's frontiers are variegated with limitless possibilities to transform the culture of fear and terror to a new culture of sustainable peace and development. In other words, if A, B, C and X, Y, Z, contextualized within I, I, I as postulated earlier (Figure 8.1), posit SPsy as a discipline that unravels the parameters, principles and promises of a new frontier of knowledge. Social psychologists have traditionally studied their behaviours and internalized norms in relation to interpersonal relationships and interactions in situations that are crucial to unravel feelings, attitudes, beliefs, cognitions, persuasions and motivations. Post-War developments in behavioural sciences underscored the significance of such an approach with emphases on individual (American) and group (Continental) dynamics. Thus intra- and interpersonal contacts, relationships and social–psychological interfaces constitute the main realm of SP.

Sigmund Freud is dated. Karl Marx is dead. Mao Tse Dong is diminished. Gandhi and Buddha have become irrelevant. Ideology that once tainted intellectual discourse has now become pragmatic and functional. However, race, religion, class and gender continue to fuel the engines of academic discourse. Frederick Nietzsche was perhaps right: There are no facts; only interpretation. This juxtaposition of ideology, science, expedience and self-interest is perhaps the single-most factor that has shaped the *construction of social practice*, a discipline that is embedded in a diverse intellectual genealogy directed toward human experience and condition.

The fundamentals—theories, methods, issues and problems— of SPsy that have been discussed during the last 50 years include a phalanx of authors including Lindzey (1954); Hartley (1961); Backman and Secord (1966); Denzin, Lindesmith and Strauss (1975); Baron and Graziano (1991); Parker (1998) and McGuire (1999). None of these texts, however, surface on the radar of current SP horizons. A casual Google search revealed 50 most important books written on SPsy.[5] The subjects mainly included in these 'most important' books include human behaviour and social being embedded in our habits, motivation, persuasion, belief, attitudes, prejudices, likings, attractions, disliking, aggression and deviance that make us 'social animals' (Brooks 2011).

'Promiscuity and fidelity', writes *Science and Technology*, 'seem to be specific biological adaptations. And their manifestations in men and women are not as different as you might expect' (*The Economist* 2015, February 3–17: 75). Human sexual behaviours, mores and mating strategies constitute a new horizon on a primordial need to survive. SP must embrace such frontiers with greater sensitivity than attributed before. Man 'has to be promiscuous (which will promote caddishness). But humans are unusual in that a father often helps care

---

[5] http://www.sparringmind.com (accessed on 23 January 2015).

for his offspring. Those offsprings are (at least, on a state of nature) less likely to survive and thrive without him. That will promote caddishness' (*The Economist* 2015, February 3–17: 75).

Modernity, innovation and technology will play havoc with traditional mores, values and patterns. Look, how smartphones and social media have changed institutional needs and behaviours. Their impact transcends personal–instinctual boundaries. ISIS is using new technologies to re-establish medieval institutions including slavery, crucifixion and beheadings as given mandates of Caliphate. Any apostate is liable to be punished in line with the religious doctrines of war. Graeme Wood writes, 'Nearly all Islamic state's decisions adhere to what it calls, on its billboards, license plates, and coins, "The Prophetic Methodology"' (2015: 83).

Our culture wars often are extended–reflective ramifications of human conflicts and conundrums that validate socio-biogenic bases of human propensities, proclivities and perceptions. One can witness cultural warriors practically in every departmental unit on a university campus that allows dissent and diversity but ignores una-bashed bigotry against the marginalized people of colour, LGBT, Jews and 'aliens' denigrated as apostates of an established order. It is doubly disturbing when an 'oppressed' individual or group play *Uncle Tom*.

There are psychosocial imperatives, which ought to be taken into serious consideration. SP has a much larger burden than psychology has claimed. What if I contend that the real cause of American longevity is more an outcome of its prosperity, level of living standards and better health care? Does it not imply than HSD are functionally intertwined and materially determined by institutional–structural factors? This reality is what I propose to be the most fascinating and challenging frontier for all social practitioners.

Sex and war have been intrinsically embedded in the history of human evolution (Hayden and Potts 2008). Since the nature of human conflict has apparently broadened beyond the territorial imperative, one cannot ignore the roots and consequences of war. Pacifism, realism and jingoism have not substantially reduced the dangers of war in a world that is increasingly better equipped to prevent and perpetuate world conflicts. This paradox of modernity involves a nexus of *social* and *psychological* determinants that call for new interpretations of old trappings.

Ian Parker aptly says, 'We *must* separate the world from our knowledge of it' (1998: xii). Social constructionist's view of reality is a non-essentialist, pragmatic approach to all human interactions and relationships. How objective is this relativist method? Can SPsy be empirically valid? These concerns posit ontological dimensions of experience in both discursive and scientific contexts.

'The terrible loneliness growing up on America', as Robert Putman puts in his new book *Our Kids: American Dream in Crisis* (2015),[6] is a manifestation of the hiatus that divides rich kids from the poor ones with immeasurable social–psychological consequences. Racial and economic inequalities compound the misery of the underprivileged, single-parent families who are pushed to the edge of survival. The myth of 'culture of poverty' still prevails in the minds of the policymakers and public. I reiterate its moral–analytical opposite: It is the *poverty of culture* that sustains dysfunctional social institutions (Mohan 2011).

SPsy's day of redemption has come to weld perceptions with reality. In domestic and international arenas, a corroded structure of communications divides peoples and nations from each other. It is hard to repair a rusty social fabric of society when race, class, gender continue to dehumanize marginalized people. Education, health care, opportunities matter. The bedrock of a civil society rests on sustainable human conditions bereft of fear, insecurity and injustice that demonize 'the others' in obsessive–compulsive systems of tyrannies of mistrust fuelled by bigoted persuasions. 12 August 2017, Charlottesville, VI: Hate and bigotry erupted as white supremacists and neo-Nazis forced declaration of emergency. Even after 70 years of democratic rule,

---

[6] http://www.washingtonpost.com/blogs/wonkblog/wp/2015/03/06/the-terrible-loneliness-of-growing-up-poor-in-robert-putnams-america/ (accessed on 7 March 2015).

India remains blighted by rabid nationalism and ethnic violence from Kashmir to Kanyakumari.[7]

Society as a whole is the quintessential lab for theoretical and experimental social psychological inquiry and research. The scope and nature of subjects within individual–societal spectrum is boundless.

> Recent debates about human shields in the summer bombardment of Gaza raised the question of how the unarmed human form comes to be regarded as a military instrument. … To what extent does the racialized structure of the visual field become instrumental to justifying the unjustifiable?[8]

The continued duality of micro–macro experience and approach has impeded SP's potential strengths to resolve variegated issues in a complex world. In a counter-intuitive culture, institutional dysfunctionality breeds intolerance, anxiety and fear. The rebirth of an *insane society* is a logical conclusion. Constructive SPsy will go a long way to salvage an otherwise catastrophic situation.

In sum, social *practice* is presented as an anti-essentialist professional disciplinarity—within the social–scientific realm—to replace antiquated vocabularies of social welfare, work and policy. Foucauldian 'archaeology' served as a guiding framework to delineate and define the *contours of transformative science* that is embedded in knowledge, value analytics and varied SPs.

'The science of man', David Hume wrote, 'is the only solid foundation for the other sciences' ([1739]1961: xiii). The search for a method has yielded interventions and practices to relate to the mysteries of human nature and its vicissitudes. The Enlightenment 'laid the basis for nothing less than a fully "secular" theodicy: a program for analyzing and remedying the evils that befall man in society' (Becker 1968: 31).

Humanity continues to be plagued by societal evils. Our SPsy and their corresponding scientific disciplines have evolved over time as

---

[7] https://www.yahoo.com/news/seventy-years-india-blighted-rabid-105107810.html (accessed on 14 August 2017).

[8] http://www.lse.ac.uk/newsAndMedia/videoAndAudio/channels/public LecturesAndEvents/player.aspx?id=2859 (accessed on 15 February 2015).

different modes of interventions in response to various issues that call for attention. Evaluative standards, hallmarks of Western political philosophy, in Foucault's interpretation, are such abstraction, first principles that we apply to validate social conditions. I intend to examine how some of these standards help us validate the authenticity of SW within social welfare.

If the Kantian *critique* flourished in Enlightenment, the latter 'is the age of critique' (Rabinow 1984: 38). Kant saw two uses of reason: private and public. Man is a cog in the machine, when reason is used for private use. Soldiers, servants, CEOs and scientists and engineers that follow a top-down order populate techno-industrial society. Their hubris and its societal impact are incalculable. When reason is put to public use, it becomes a servant of humanity and a champion of freedom. In other words, public and private uses of reason correspond to freedom and oppression (Mohan 1985; 1986). 'There is Enlightenment when the universal, the free, and the public uses of reason are superimposed on one another' (Rabinow 1984: 37).

Degrees of Inequalities and the viability of the *American Dream* are incompatible. Suzanne Mettler (2014) implicates higher education as a saboteur. Her 'important book documents the destructive forces in higher education, forces fostered and nurtured by a Congress that has abdicated responsibility to ensure the strengths of this country's most important engine of social mobility' (Edsall 2014).[9] Now that higher education is in a mess, disciplines outside the mission ring will either be cannibalized or eliminated. SW programmes found a safe haven on campuses due to their market value and low-cost investment.

Now that technical, digital, business and growth-oriented departmental units are attracting endowments and grants, soft disciplines are paying price for their 'softness'. Information revolution has changed the way of life. SW never could authenticate its value to the scientific

[9] Thomas B. Edsall quoted in the *New York Review of Books* LXI, no. 9 (22 May 2014): 3. I have successfully and unsuccessfully published a number of letters on the crisis of higher education with the same contention. How could a system practise and produce social justice when it is essentially designed to breed inequality?

community. Mere feckless licensing does not legitimize authenticity. A professional devolution does not happen without a reason.

The Inconvenient Truths

Environment cannot be isolated from the cultural and economic superstructure of values, services and technologies. The environmental toxicity is largely attributable to many a man-made problem over which they have lost control. For example, take Wall Street—the nerve centre of world capitalism. At one point—not too long ago—a few hedge fund-owners managed 3 trillion US dollars until FBI investigated the scandal. Rajratnam, the first big shark arrested, lived so flamboyantly that he flew 70 friends to Kenya for a birthday safari. Steven Cohen, one of the richest men in the world, 'plans to reopen his hedge fund as soon as possible' (Kolhatkar 2017: 295). In other words, 'greed is good' creed is inseparable from the quest of success. This imperative deepens the 1 per cent and 99 per cent divide to the extent that inequality and humanity seem inseparable. Then, what happened to social justice?

Educational programmes, institutional philanthropy and altruistic services—all dependent on endowments, grants, state support and individual charities—cannot achieve social justice. Their primary goal is not achieving equality. SW as a profession is guilty of hiding this cruel truth from its students and 'clients' who are routinely 'hedged',[10] metaphorically, by pricey schools and shoddy institutions.[11, 12]

[10] Sheela Kolhatkar in her *Black Edge* (2017) offers a thriller-like view of Wall Street. In one sentence, she reveals a very unsettling spectacle of our environment: 'Being long some stocks and short others meant that you were "hedged." This strategy could be applied to other financial instruments in addition to stocks, such as bonds and options and futures, in any market in the world' (2017: xvi).

[11] 'There is a perception that in the years after Milkmen era, and especially after the financial crisis of 2018, it has become almost impossible, due to lack of will or expertise, to prosecute corporate ceremonials who operate at the highest levels' (Kolhatkar 2017: 294). One might question my logic to treat corporate criminals at par with educational, scientific, technological institutions. The point I make, however, is—power elites are beyond law. This lawlessness is inherently hostile to the powerless people who seek justice.

[12] There is moral crisis in Silicon Valley. https://finance.yahoo.com/news/why-freada-kapor-klein-thinks-163003319.html?.tsrc=fauxdal (accessed on 8 October 2017).

Al Gore 'can whip out his cell phone and dial the treasury secretary or the head of a giant solar panel manufacturer and say things such as, "I'll check with President Hollande" or "Elon suggested I call"'. This is the power of his Inconvenient Sequel.[13] Melting glaciers and rising oceanic temperatures—the climate change—is an undeniable reality. Evangelizing against the plausible ominous end is the finest example of SP.

---

[13] https://www.theguardian.com/film/2017/jan/20/an-inconvenient-sequel-review-al-gore-climate-change-documentary (accessed on 30 July 2017).

CHAPTER 9

Freedom and Vocabularies of Change

This chapter is a microcosm of my work: It seeks to anthologize in context the main constructs and concepts that undergird my modest effort to unravel the dialectics of freedom in an unfree world. During the past five decades at least, I have endeavoured to comprehend the complexity of a phenomenon that I still find perplexing.

There is no zero-sum game in between freedom and oppression (unfreedom). As Herbert Marcuse said, one can be free even at the hands of his executioner. One can be unfree even at the pinnacle of power.

A decade ago, a few decent friends asked me to bring out a book that would highlight major conceptual contributions. Modesty foreboded my interest. However, I yielded when two colleagues of mine helped me to identify the key concepts and notions that warrant a focused location in the whole trajectory of my writings.[1]

---

[1] I self-published *Society and Social Justice: A Nexus in Review*. Before I collected certain gleanings and musings, I methodologically classified these in five major sections. By and large, I present here the crux of a 'nexus' that would help readers to glance through the whole spectrum of issues. For the sake of originality, I shall confine to the scope and confines of *Society and Social Justice* (2012).

Friendly AI will make future safer. Many question this optimism. Nonetheless, integrated disciplinarity may have something to look for. I offer only a social scientist's perspective that is concerned about human trappings in the first place.

This chapter offers cross-sectional analytic indicators to my life's work. The multilinearity of certain issues that run through an opus is carefully combed to situate the essence of a protean trajectory encompassing an array of issues broadly classified in five thematic areas. It is a self-reflective anthology of my views, constructs and conceptions of varied social phenomena and realities.

This anthological compilation in this chapter might serve as a *Brij Mohan Reader* connecting the conceptual dots of a rather complex system of thought. Since most of my books are solo monographs, their universal availability all at once is an unrealistic expectation for students and teachers who look for appropriate citation from the original sources.

To the best my knowledge, there is no such book on a range of intertwined subjects by a single thinker–educator in our field. As such, no existing anthology or reader in SW and social welfare compares this volume. Some of the quotes embody my 'eureka' moments; several others were brought to my attention by students and friends, mainly Lilly Allen, S. Zafar Hasan, K.S. Soodan and Usha Srivastava.

A thematic approach looked feasible despite the overlapping nature of certain concepts and constructs that I usually allude to. A simple taxonomy of this chapter is vaguely organized around a constellation of five major sections. Each part opens with a semi-autobiographical narrative that substantiates the ethos of human conditions.

The Human Condition

* Freedom
* Alienation
* Caste and casteism
* Mental illness
* Oppression

- Exclusions
- Violence and counter-violence
- Terror

Theoretico-philosophical Streams

- Existentialism
- Buddhist and Vedic thoughts
- Freudo-Marxist endowment
- Logical humanism

Social Constructs and Interventions

- Social transformation
- Social work, practice, problems, policy, welfare and action
- Social contract II

International Aspects and Issues

- New internationalism
- International society
- International SW
- Comparative social welfare
- Social policy
- Social development
- International conflict and war
- South Asia
- World peace and coexistence

Science, Society and Values

- Unification of science
- Humanistic positivism
- Ideology and dystopia
- Democracy
- Culture and chaos
- Poverty of culture

Methodology

This will allow readers to locate and access appropriate themes from most of my publications listed here. If developed into a comprehensive system, the quantum of analyses might help future of social work and social policy. As a substitute for this future possibility, this chapter will serve as a guide to explore the dynamic and interconnectedness of sociocultural and psychological phenomena.

The five categories reflect on numerous human conditions in a paradigmatic way. There is no rational basis for creating these separate sections as it tends to fracture the very basis of wholeness and holistic thinking. However, we made these taxonomical subsections and categories to spread out distinct but related subjects from a pragmatic standpoint.

Since most of the citations are quoted from 16 of my books, the references given parenthetically only refer to year of publication and page numbers. This will eliminate the formal requirement of repeatedly citing the same author's name and the associated monotony. For example, if there is a quote from *Development, Poverty of Culture and Social Policy* (*DPoC&SP*), its corresponding citation will appear in parenthesis as (*DPoC&SP* 2011: page number/s). A few significant sources beyond these books have been appropriately footnoted.

The Human Condition

> *What I call* le vécu *is the accumulation of the dialectical process of psychic life insofar as this process remains obscure to itself as a constant totalization. It is impossible to be conscious of a totalization, which also totalizes consciousness.* Le vécu, *in this sense, is permanently susceptible of comprehension but never of knowledge.*
> —Jean-Paul Sartre (quoted by his biographer, Hayman 1987: 431)

Le vécu offered me a new critical perspective to comprehend and think outside the box. The human condition, thus, has been the general foundation I have built up my basic conceptual frameworks. In doing so, Franco-German thoughts, especially continental philosophy, has been my main intellectual endowment. While Gandhian thought has guided my moral orientation, it is Sartrean ethics that has been my intellectual model to comprehend and analyze different aspects and issues relative to human conditions.

While sensitive to the oppression of the poor and downtrodden, especially Dalits in India, I began scientific exploration of more serious subjects like mental illness soon after my master's education in SW (1960).

Michel Foucault's 'madness' escaped me until the mid-1990s under the eclipse of my Freudian loyalties. But when I finally came to know his archaeology of knowledge, I found him to be a Sartrean kin. After publishing a book and so many pieces of my doctoral research, I realized the phony dichotomy between mental sanity and insanity, a false duality institutionalized by the DSM architects.

I found the world outside mental institutions much more chaotic and sick (1972, 1973). This conviction has evolved in a new theory of 'Poverty of Culture' (Mohan 2011), which unravels the dynamics of our cultural meltdowns. My search for freedom, encompassing unfreedoms unleashed by oppressive cultures and predatory institutions, continues. A 'comparative–analytic' framework (1985a, 1985b) helps me situate and interconnect spatio-temporal 'dots' beyond the disciplinarities of dated dogmas.

> When irrationality is wedded to arrogance, stupidity is born.... I would argue that the dichotomy of developed and developing nations is a meaningless absurdity.... A new consciousness to deconstruct the existing culture of violence, alienation, and institutional–individual narcissism calls for a paradigm shift that essentially boils down to certain basic rules of civility. A responsible society must promote and sustain the elemental humanity of each individual and community. This seems to be better and perhaps the only way to transform the world.
>
> (Mohan 2011c: 74–77)

> When certain individuals and groups are subjected to unkind beliefs (isms) and unfair practices (discrimination), ideology becomes a tool of oppression. Nazism of the nadir of this behavior.... While

prejudice is prejudged negative attitude, discrimination is an act of villainy. Both serve as tools in the oppressive hands of a perpetrator who discriminate others on the basis of caste, class, race, gender, age, origin, and beliefs.

(*Eclipse of Freedom* [*EoF*] 1993: 56)

Our belief systems generate the ideologies of freedom and oppression.... When a person or a class of persons act(s) as perpetrator(s).... we speak of an oppressive situation.... When societal institutions become barriers of equality and justice—the two guardians of true freedom (Mohan, 1988)—human oppression becomes pervasive evil. In brief, this is the anatomy of unfreedom.

(*EoF* 1993: 56–57)

Dimensions of human freedom and unfreedom constitute the crux of all human conditions. Freedom is an awesome responsibility and unfreedom is a vicious trap. Man's enslavement is an outcome of his own needs, trappings, and artifacts.

(*Denial of Existence* [*DoE*] 1987: 3)

Human conditions are adaptations to social reality over which mortals have lost control. Science and technology have ceased to be—perhaps they never were!—liberating forces. Civilization is a slaughterhouse. Commercialization of the cosmos has cost the scientists and the universe the ultimate value: Human dignity.

(*DoE* 1987: 3)

The analysis of the human condition transcends the rigid premises of behaviorism, scientism, and system-oriented perspectives because objectivity, quantification and value-freedom do not adequately explain the nature and dimension of human suffering.... Experience, consciousness, and wholeness are essential ingredients of human conditions that determine the nature of existence as lived through differential processes. Behavioral sciences, in their reliance on quantification and mathematical rigor, represent a flight from [human] reality.

(*DoE* 1987: 5)

Existential intervention is conceptualized here as a viable outlook for the alleviation of human suffering in a self-creative dialectical process. It helps rebuild the impaired identity.... It highlights one fundamental value: the impairing of self is remediable through an existential process involving realistic self-appraisal, awareness and actualization, directional-reorientation, and experiential-cognitive modes.... A new principle in existential social work is formulated: it brings into focus a therapeutic quest for the emergence of an integrative identity beyond the client-centered systems.

(*DoE* 1987: 28)

Domestic violence is kind of silent social plague; its dimensions are complex and staggering. Vanishing familial ties, across cultural and regional boundaries, represent the malaise of the ailing social systems. A wounded family corrodes societal conscience.

(*DoE* 1987: 61)

Asylum-like horrid conditions of the mental hospitals at work, appalling magnitude of mental ills, staggering lack of proper therapeutic programs, callously negative community attitudes towards the poor insane and—above all—the general socio-economic conditions of a painfully acquisitive feudally oriented system, present both a challenge and an opportunity to all those concerned with the task of nation-building to work out a rationally conceived integrated plan of action inspired with a progressive ideology directed toward the welfare of the mentally ill in India.

(*Social Psychiatry in India* [*SPiI*] 1973: 2)

... [M]ental illness and mental health are not absolute conditions; the former becomes distinguishable when the desired attributes of the latter appear disappearing. While impairment affecting role and status calling for psychiatric attention helps us define mental illness, personal maturity marked by adequate socio-personal adjustment, integration, self-restraint, reality orientation and cultural adaptability enables the identification of positive attributes that characterize mental health. In social psychiatry both conditions need to be studied in togetherness. This opens unlimited vistas of collaboration between the psychiatrist and the social scientist.

(*SPiI* 1973: 13)

Caste system, the fundamental rhythm of Indian life, is the genesis of casteism and untouchability. ... Indeed, it is a basis of social stratification.... The division of human groups on the basis of disposition, character and capacity is a general characteristic of most societies, particularly those feudally stratified. Caste in India seems to be the essence of social structure and its survival as its all-pervasive influence characterizes the very Indian way of life.

(*India's Social Problems* [*ISP*] 1972: 21)

The revolt of Harijans[2] appears imminent against the tyranny of the high castes.... The provision of reserved constituency for scheduled castes is a calculated attempt to keep the lower castes divided amongst themselves. A faction-ridden community would find it well neigh impossible to win over its enemy. It is a greater challenge for the Harijans; their dilemma will continue unless they rid themselves of bourgeoization. This is, however, a revolutionary task and [it] cannot be accomplished with mere obsessive notions and slogans.... To eradicate casteism and untouchability a caste war has to be fought no doubt but its ideology and program of action should be objectively progressive. It would be self-defeating and nationally devastating to resort to reactionary methods and thinking.[3]

(*ISP* 1972: 27, 28–29)

The eclipse of civility spells the dualism of despair and hope. Human oppression is an inescapable experience. The pain of hunger is no more a Third World curse; scourges of poverty and authoritarianism are pervasive. Even the most advanced nations in the world are not immune to the ravages of the new poverty—a phenomenon that marks the failure of the post-industrial society in meeting common human needs.

(*EoF* 1993: xi)

Oppression has no identity; it's the ugly name of a feckless behavior born out of human rapaciousness, compulsions, and manipulative

---

[2] 'Dalit' is now a preferred concept to refer to all oppressed lower castes including the 'scheduled' ones.

[3] The prescience of these observations is, however, notable. The revolt of the Dalit has changed the contours of national politics. A state like Uttar Pradesh, which was lately ruled by a 'Dalit' woman, Mayawati, is reflective of a widespread corruption of 'revolutionary praxis'. India's current caste war is reactionary at best.

power which I prefer to call predatory politics. Equally, perhaps more, indomitable is the human urge to breathe the fresh air of freedom.

(*EoF* 1993: xi)

The triumph of global capitalism is sadly based on the every-man-for-himself doctrine. Amid the ambiguities of the twentieth century post-war climate one finds that brutality still works. The archaic elements of human nature still regulate the conduct, which falls short of civilized behavior. However, the only organizing principle that keeps the societal cauldron from spilling [over] seems to be the powerlessness of the oppressed people. How else could one explain the invincibility of the authority of whose legitimacy remains in question? The state benefits from, and depends on, the functional rationale of its coercive power.

(*EoF* 1993: xii)

The ravages of postmodern crisis challenge the development and education of the human animal—an incomplete creature in search of a meaningful identity. Exploration of this unfreedom is but a step toward becoming universally free.

(*EoF* 1993: xii)

Despite a nebulous description, human oppression remains an encompassing ontological reality.... Human experience as a datum merits a phenomenological inquiry should oppression be the prism of policy directions. Societal institutions have traditionally sought to safeguard human dignity against the vagaries of nature and individual-social circumstances. Frequently, however, social arrangements and human nature fail to promote freedom and become tools of oppression. Human struggle for, and beyond, survival is a perennial saga of liberation from the innate trappings and external barriers.

(*EoF* 1993: xv)

Our social world is a smorgasbord of human duality; its paradoxes and contradictions signify the intersection between rational and irrational, external and temporal, material and metaphysical.

(*EoF* 1993: xv)

Racism is as American as apple pie. Hostility and contempt based on the color of human skin is not a new phenomenon, however. India's 'varnavyavastha'—system based on color—the cornerstone of 'casteism', is a primal form of racism that has sustained the egalitarian reforms of a modern democracy.

(*EoF* 1993: 57)

Theoretico-philosophical Streams

My father was a physician, philosopher and philanthropist—a dangerous combination that permeated his rise and fall as a worldly man. However, above all, he was a wise and noble human being. Though we lived in relative poverty, despite his good medical practice, ancestral assets and his creative mind, our values with empathetic orientation and altruistic attitudes transformed my whole view of material wealth and its significance. All property is a theft—looked to be a very accurate definition and source of inequality, as I understood as a young student. The morality of both the Wall Street and Silicon Valley validates my then nascent *judgementality*.

In this family milieu of modest means and a heightened sense of morality, I grew up as a rebel with a cause. When throngs of impoverished patients arrived early morning at my father's clinic with their dying infants, I realized there was something terribly wrong somewhere. Why only poor ones had to suffer on account of misery for which they were not responsible? For a while, I followed my father's philosophy of karma and dharma but it did not help me much. As soon as I began to develop my own sense of ethics, I realized how hollow our religious practices were. In one of our earliest family visits to the temples of Vrindavan, I noted how Dalits were excluded from entrance. I plainly told my father that I questioned the moral authority of a god who will distinguish between classes and castes of human beings. My journey had begun on a rather tedious track. After graduation, I joined MSW, a new programme at Agra University. My sense of social work then was more pragmatic than philosophical. It was my assumption that MSWs would be the next messiahs of social change as India was embarking upon a massive national social development programme through her Five Years Plans.

I moved to Lucknow University to benefit from the tutelage of celebrated scholars at a prestigious university, a pioneer in SW doctoral educational research. It offered me the opportunity to explore human conditions which were dearest and nearest to my inquisitive mind. The fieldwork involved interviewing and observing hospitalized mental patients in the three mental hospitals of North India (Uttar Pradesh). To date, that experience stands out as the peak of my learning. The more I knew about mental illness, the less I knew about 'normal' human behaviour. With humility and sustained interest, I continue to explore human dimensions of social misery without a convincing recipe for radical transformation. As a natural evolutionary process, in my quest for a paradigm that unfolds dynamics of difficult issues, I continue to seek answers to knotty questions with a sense of philosophical hope. If this sounds escapist, I offer my apology. I have to believe that practising ethical norms with philosophical approach to personal and social problems serves both as a tranquilizer and prophylaxis for undue pain and unwarranted anguish. This approach does not help you to fight corruption and stop genocide; this does help you to practise hope with a creative attitude in an otherwise chaotic world.

If social and natural scientists would embrace each other without orthodoxies of their calling, theoretical–scientific interpretations would tremendously enhance the cause of human liberation. It is not ignorance; it is the arrogance of the learned that worries me most. Anti-dialogic disciplinarities sabotage knowledge and its impact. A philosophical orientation is crucial to relate to others, the 'others' whom we tend to neglect, abuse, dread and hate. When I say there is only one race, that is, the human race, I behold humanity as a family, which has become dysfunctional owing to our misunderstandings.

Some of the relevant constructs that represent these formulations are best analyzed and discussed in three specific books: *Global Development: Post-Material Values and Social Praxis* (1992), *The Practice of Hope* (2003) and *Metaphysics of Social Practice* (2005).

We must first look inside the box before we reconnect the dots outside the box.

(*Journal of Comparative Social Work* [*JCSW*] 2012: 78)

The main burden of these musings is to underscore the foundational significance of post-Nietzschean–Darwinian–Sartrean streams of thought that have deconstructed the meaning of *being* and *becoming* as a paradigm shift in our understanding of human nature and behavior.... I believe *postmodern* is a misnomer.... The rise of anti-Platonism lent support to anti-essentialism, which has helped develop postmodern thought in arts, humanities and literature. In social/human services, its impact has been monumental without a clearer understanding of its meaning, implication, and impact.

(*Journal of Social Work Education* [*JSWE*] 2011: 620–624)

Optimism without an empathetic sense of reality is an apology to cultivated somnambulism. The post-industrial society—in the throes of a variegated crisis—is like an orphan, if not aborted, child whose mother [modernity] did not get the midwife's help.

(*EoF* 1993: 5)

Human Society, Social Constructs and Interventions

The construction of social reality is a phenomenal abstraction that impinges upon human and social behaviours in varied manifestations. Our responses and patterns of cultural reactions institutionalize this continual strife in linear and multilinear manner. Both individual and society follow an evolutionary trajectory until a cataclysmic change is encountered due to social, economic or natural upheaval of historic proportions.

A revolution is, by definition, a radical intervention to bring out a change. Its outcome is both unpredictable and challenging. Social transformation may and may not be a by-product of revolution. What recent history suggests is that revolution itself is in an evolutionary phase. From Bolshevik Revolution to the Arabian Spring, we witness varied uprisings with unreliably different outcomes. Since *change* is the constant with universal validity, I have ventured to explore this reality in different contexts.

When I became a student of SW in 1958, I had envisioned a professional intervention to be the Holy Grail of desired social change. In principle, my innate belief still holds water. What did not transpire is the 'self-fulfilling prophecy' as revolutions devour their own children. Even the forces of the Enlightenment did not bring out the Age of Reason. I have hypothesized that much of our social malaise is on account of the demise of 'social contract'. I have pleaded for the Enlightenment II to see that a new social contract does insure a better world devoid of ignorance, poverty and violence.

> Social policy is viewed here as societal response to historico-political injustices that have been inflicted on humanity in the name of dogmas a free society cannot accept. Now that the 'darkest' century is behind us, we must embark upon a new age of innovative directions with hope for a better world. (Mohan 2011: 95–107)
>
> (*Journal of Policy Practice* [*JPP*] 2011: 95)

> Policy innovations, by intent and definition, are progressive directions toward change—social change that ameliorates poverty and heals the wounds of an unjust feudal, colonial and imperial past. Globalization, after all, failed to be the patina of cross-national democracies.
>
> There would be no need for any policy innovation if human society were an impeccable system. Since we live in a less than perfect world, intellectuals, especially policy thinkers and practitioners, must reflect on and build upon individual and collective experiences that will insure a better world for our posterity.
>
> (*JPP* 2011: 96)

> India's advancements aside, its entropic public corruption, a primitive bureaucracy and nearly chaotic politics must be good news to its nemesis…. India's 4,000 km long borders with two hostile neighbors in cahoots with each other cannot expect Gandhian passivity from India while they themselves pursue aggressive policies. China's one-party government offers coercive social policy framework, which is a contradiction in terms. Social policy is quintessentially a democratic response to societal needs. But democratic freedom, like India's, is a monstrosity that muffles any hope for constructive development.
>
> (*JPP* 2011: 98)

SW as a profession is a twentieth century American innovation. Its evolution is a mark of the rise of the Welfare State. These states of welfare institutionalized residual functions and ensured people security against the contingencies of modernity. The twenty-first century realities are starkly daunting and different. We notice meltdowns in our basic social, economic, and political institutions. The troubled manifestations of these cultural crises are beyond the SW-EPR purview, competencies and even imagination. The 'rest of the world' is emulating the American model, which is inherently dated. This is internationalizing a flawed model of education, which is so vitally important in a newly global world. A truly *postmodern* approach to problem solving implies radical changes in program and curricular structures, pedagogies, epistemologies of change. ([*DPoc&SP*] Mohan 2011d)

The organization of SW theory, practice as a field, method and process is largely the outcome of the Western sociological 'imagination' embedded in the systems theory. My research in the field suggests that the organization of social welfare system and its functions are primarily guided by Parsonsian theory of action, which we do not teach at all these days. I am no fan of Parsons' macro-functionalism; yet, silver-plating an old vessel with postmodernist polish is no justice to either theory and/or practice. ([*DPoC&SP*] Mohan 2011) (*JSWE* 2011: 622)

> 'Obsolescence of social work' is premised on the notion that 'person in social environment'—the object—has become obsolescent [in reality].... The dissociation of human and social realities is an outcome of professional politics. A sense of rediscovery is essential to achieve a synthesis.... Unification, universalization, and demythologization of knowledge, values, fields, and methods are necessary processes to regenerate social work's vitality, identity, and legitimacy.
>
> (*EoF* 1993: 108, 110)

> Social policy must be conceptualized as a liberating mechanism directed toward social justice.
>
> (*EoF* 1993: 116)

If the roots of social policy lie in the social contract thesis, the determinants of human behavior ought to be explored in an evolutionary framework. The concept of interpersonal human behavior, beyond the Judeo-Christian-Moslem conformity and Freudo-Marxist determinism, has come of age: ward of anxiety and preserve self-esteem.

(New Horizons in Social Welfare and Policy [*NHSW&P*] 1985a: 133)

[There] is a new horizon for policy analysts and theorists. The world realities of contemporary cultures and political systems dictate that each nation move to a progressive direction to become a dynamic whole of the universe. Our unconsciousness of this reality will amount to a self-destructive illusion.

(*NHSW&P* 1985a: 134)

Comparative social welfare seeks to analyze attributive variables of welfare systems across the board: it attempts to unravel human conditions, policies, institutions, values. Resources, methodologies and delivery systems of various societies, portraying differential dimensions of and approaches to complex social issues and problems.

(*Toward Comparative Social Welfare* [*TCSW*] 1985b: 1)

Comparative welfare, by its definition and nature, cannot be a value-free endeavor since varied societal conditions and arrangements are studied within a framework that is built upon humanistic, universal and transcendental values. If social misery, for example, is the focus of a comparative study, it implies a critical–evaluative approach to the analysis of historico-societal forces (feudalism, colonialism, imperialism, fascism, etc.,) that have caused global ill fare.

(*TCSW* 1985b: 2)

Since human behavior, social welfare, social progress, scientific developments and global wellbeing cannot be—in fact, should not be—dealt within culturally isolated pockets, comparative analysis [becomes] a viable means for *unification* of fragmented theories and approaches that concern universal wellbeing.

(*TCSW* 1985b: 3)

The method of comparing is perhaps the oldest human endeavor that led to empirical and experimental inquiry. We compare and judge; evaluate and asset; distinguish and validate—all in the process of authenticity that rejects and accepts certain assumptions and concepts leading to theories and generalization. Basic assumptions underlying this framework are threefold:

- Human commonalities, despite vast differences, constitute a system of unity that may be called universal humanity.
- Mutual understanding and awareness is a positive strategy for establishing endurable relations with interacting others (groups, societies, and nations).
- An intelligent and sincere assessment of the world situation (forces, conditions, and relations) suggest that global welfare is prerequisite to cross-national harmony and order. (*TCSW* 1985b: 4)[4]

A decolonized society with an aversion to progressive social change, rampant with political corruption, becomes a fertile field for the mushroom growth of divisive and disruptive forces.... While stress, restlessness, anxiety and insecurity grow in general, disparity between haves and have-nots and the gap between principles and practices internally decompose the entire system.

(*ISP* 1972: 106–107)

International Aspects and Issues

The notion of 'universal family' (*Vasudhaivakutambhkum*) existed long before I wrote about an *international society* or, abstractly, globalization became a common word. Contemporary societies are glued together

---

[4] These basic, underlying assumptions of 'comparative social welfare' constitute the structure of a 'comparative–analytic' framework that has inspired many a formulation but without due acknowledgment. Comparative social welfare's (CSW) misfortune has been that it is neither well understood nor duly appreciated by those who need it most. It is my belief, CSW must be included in the foundational courses of all master's, doctoral level offerings in social sciences in general, and social work, welfare and policy in particular. CSW is a valid, viable and crucial method and perspective in international social work (ISW). It is unfortunate 'US-based' ISW remains expediently non-cognizant of its own origins.

in a whole, which are fraught with territorial imperatives and fissures of self-interests. Modern nationalities remain barbarously primitive when it comes to reason with a neighbour. Israel and Palestine, or India and Pakistan, are excellent examples where fires of hell have been alight ever since their birth.

I did not invent 'international social work' as some of my critics have claimed for themselves. Since I have a cross-national upbringing and transnational education in SW, the cause and rationale for internationalizing SW has been dear to me. I published my research on mental health in *International Social Work* before I came to the United States. However, in this land of freedom, I have seldom seen a field as narrow as 'US-based' SW. The painful truth that even our CSWE has endorsed this view is unfortunate and regrettable.

About 25 years ago, Ramesh Mishra and I talked about writing something on social welfare with a global framework. Since we both are solo writers, we published our books on the subjects independently but with mutual respect. *Global Development: Post-Material Values and Social Praxis* (Mohan 1992) grew out of a paper that I presented in Lima, Peru at the 25th International Congress of Schools of Social Work (15–20 August 1990). The subtitle of the book was the main burden of my paper, which, to my utter surprise, received an overwhelming response in Latin America. Again, when I visited Brazil and Chile two decades later I received similar responses. This convinced me that 'US-based' approach is fundamentally hegemonic[5] and fraught with individual–institutional narcissism. There is no room for such trappings in a noble profession like ours. Alas, I am not that optimistic any more.

> Internationalism is premised on a global consciousness which can be both hegemonic as well as egalitarian.... Social development must be compatible with progress. Acquisition and progress are not analogous concepts (88). Globalization of market economy, privatization of human services, and individualization of social needs seem to thwart the possibility of a sustainable culture.

[5] Sonia Kapur's review of *Trans-national Social Work Practice*.

A nexus of forces calls into question the validity and efficacy of social development as a method. A diverse and pluralistic world is being torn apart by the ravages of ethnic, sectarian and neo-imperialist violence (90).... Democratization and social development are interdependent processes.... Developmental perspective is fraught with issues that concern three areas of major concern: (1) Third Worldization of development; (2) globalization of conflict; and (3) new worldization of order (94).

(*EoF* 1993: 88–94)

Economic nationalism, ethnocentric militarism, xenophobia, and world capitalism are bound *to create multipolar superpowers* embedded with corporate rapaciousness. The impact of this neoglobal climate is unlikely to change to foster peace and justice in the world community. Social development and its life-sustaining thrusts can serve two functions: it can be an 'alibi' for perpetuating the post-industrial perversity; it can also become a casualty of the post-industrial society. In either instance, social development as a world project shared by all national communities as a universally accepted model of global welfare is unlikely to emerge a 'bioglobal' paradigm (Mohan 1988) of hope and dignified coexistence.

(*EoF* 1993: 95–96; emphasis added)[6]

Science, Values and Social Reality

It is a Faustian science, and within the limitations of life on earth it could propose to do great things. It is Kantian science, and a Deweyan one: it is bounded by man's limitations, and it is dependent on man's active transactions with its environment. It doesn't take over the full task of religion since anthropodicy is not a theodicy: it would limit itself to the use of human powers affecting whatever they can to overcome avoidable evil. Man would abandon otherworldly groupings for unrealistic ideals, and content to make his meanings unfold in the material, everyday world.

(Becker 1968: 376)[7]

[6] Cf. Fareed Zakaria's *The Post-American World* (2008) published 15 years after the publication of *Eclipse of Freedom* (Mohan 1993).
[7] I quote this passage from one of the best books written during the last 50 years in social sciences. Unfortunately, Becker did not get the recognition he deserved.

C. Wright Mills was right: Science is a pretentious messiah. Like a sharp knife in a surgeon or thug's hands, it can perform two opposite functions. Hence, functionality, for lack of a better word, is a cautious imperative to license any scientific advancement. However, functionality is not a value-free concept. We invaded Iraq based on lies in the name of democracy. Pakistan prides itself on its nukes designed and directed to destroy India's major centres of development. China's robust capitalism dwarfs any Western rapaciousness.

The conflict between values and science is not a new one. Objectivity, truth and general well-being have been the cornerstones of universal morality, if there is such a concept. In this century, after the horrors of its immediate predecessor, it assumes great importance to synthesize science and values. This partakes of special significance in a globalized world, which seeks to globalize democratic values and practices.

Both science and technology do not exist is a non-societal context. Societal wombs generate fears, delusions and hope. Great civilizations have disappeared—or *Collapsed*!—when disasters threatened extinction. Are we ahead to such a cataclysmic epoch? Perhaps not. The Book of Revelation was written by a spiritual pornographer. I believe in science and its cause. Science is man's greatest weapon against dogmatic heresies, which have brought nightmares and mass murders. It is incumbent on intellectuals of the world to see that fight against unreason and inhumanity is not lost. Science does not safeguard it, nor will reason. There is no dearth of great scientists and rationalists.

Humanity calls for enlightened citizenry to impact the shape and outcome of democratic processes that guide our destinies. Education is one such vehicle if properly harnessed and brilliantly imparted. Another 'heretical' pronouncement is that of annihilation of despair all around the globe, not just in the darkness of developing nations. Should policymakers, public leaders and corporate executives conveniently forget these basic mandates, it is not the bloodthirstiness of Revelation that will annihilate all of us; it will be the madness of one Dr Strangelove who will preside over a common destiny of total doom. This is not a biblical prophecy; this is a rational conclusion of an ordinary humanist who can think globally and act critically despite the clouds of inclement weather.

If the twentieth century was the age of revolutions, the twenty-first century will be remembered as a post-revolutionary era when absolutes of ideology melted away in the heat of global dynamics. The bumpy road ahead is not a hindrance; it is a challenge that we have to accept professionally and truthfully. (*JPP* 2011: 96)

The burden of post-ideological policy agenda should: (a) *de-Platonize*, (b) *humanize*, and (c) *contextualize* policy innovations as the main goal of social transformation. A search for society that is free from violence, terror and dehumanization is a continuous process. Delusional it may seem it's a paradoxical outcome of a dystopian culture that we have accepted as a bargain for unprincipled success and consumerist survival. The fundamental values of a civil society that we all seek to achieve are compromised in the process of what we call social development. The point is: social–human development should be interdependent; public and social policies ought to be congruent in this process; and world governments should strive for peaceful coexistence in the common interest of international decency, dignity, and survival. (*JPP* 2011: 99)

There is no cure for ill-diagnosed mass dementia that is often consumed with individualism, hedonism, communism and capitalism. (*International Review of Modern Sociology* [*IRMS*] 2009: 259–270)

CHAPTER 10

The End of Social Work: Epilogue

Optimal stopping is the science of serial monogamy…. Every harried renter, driver, and suitor you see around you as you go through a typical week is essentially reinventing the wheel. They don't need a therapist; they need an algorithm. The therapist tells them to find the right, comfortable balance between impulsivity and overthinking. The algorithm tells the balance is thirty-seven percent.

—Brian Christian and Tom Griffiths (2016: 2–3).

Therapy's trajectory from the cave of a primitive *shaman* to the office of a 'licensed practitioner', almost runs parallel to the zigzag trail of social evolution. Acquisition, strife and alienation lead to modernization followed by post-industrial acquisitions, affluence and their implied burdens. Commoditization of health and wellness along with the rise of post-ideological strides brought pragmatism and globalization. Pure altruism perhaps never existed. The forces of evolution morphed societal institutions into mechanism of both survival and conquest.

The baggage that global democracy and free market carry is stuffed with many illusions. Growing inequality and environmental injustices are formidable challenges that a sustainable international social order demands. Collective–idealist notions of a socialist utopia, yielding to a new way of corporate avarice, have failed humanity. A hideous cycle of consumption, compulsion and conflict has created a system that maintains a façade of civility without substance. This hydraulic system of human needs, (*things*) and (unfulfilled) existential vacuity is the cornerstone of a therapeutic society. In sum, (a) a theory of 'therapeutic culture' is in order to (b) illustrate the dialectics of madness and well-being and (c) explore pathways to overcome the painful angst on the cusp of our paradoxical progress.

SW as a suffix to any orientation serves as a pragmatic fix to forge a specialized field. From *nephrology* SW to *military* SW, a spectrum of specializations—at the expense of SW's own identity—appears like a 'jack of all trades' without much validity. Not that SP is the suggested panacea, its infusion across the disciplinarities is at least devoid of both departmentality and developmentality, the twine unmistakable burdens that contemporary SWP carries.

Social development is a contradiction in terms. Ever since the *social contract* died, the 'social' remains an impervious force, latent at best. Development is a product of modernity's quest and hubris for achieving a 'civilized' version of humanity.[1] Barbarians and savages— the underdeveloped people—have to be modernized. In West Chicago's Schools, it is a war zone. A few miles off my native village (in India), my life rewinds back to the seventeenth century. Missions and crusades are euphemisms that subjugate people robbed off their fortunes and opportunities in the cruel strife for survival. The notions implied and employed in SP offer a modest attempt to self-empower people under environmental savagery. Digital tribalism and AI may end human race. Al Gore's *Inconvenient Sequel*, on the other hand, endangers mother earth.

Conclusion

The rise of inequality and injustice call for new algorithms of social transformation to stave off an unprecedented human crisis.

---

[1] https://www.theguardian.com/social-care-network/2017/apr/07/politicians-are-stealthily-trying-to-take-control-of-social-work (accessed on 8 April 2017).

Social media and digital revolution have fundamentally changed the meanings of 'social' and 'work'. *Social work*, like all other professions, will undergo dramatic changes—may even disappear as robots overtake human operations with greater efficiency with lesser cost. The failure of social sciences in general and *social work* in particular warrants thoughtful innovations that insure sustainable services.

Contradictions of capitalism, globalization and social development have diminished the plausibility of annihilation of forces that breed inequality, injustice and oppression. The enigmatic force of 'diversity' has run its course. To counteract this dysfunctional *developmentality*, I have examined the crisis of the social welfare domain and unravelled how meltdown of institutional securities is generating a climate of angst, anger and anxiety, which is detrimental to human development.

Books and monographs in the field generally deal with the past and the present of SW practices that sustain status quo in policy, service and field experiences that cover a gamut of interrelated issues. I question the existing model of SW education; its online, expensive programmes simply undercut the foundational ideals that sustained its credibility. A new perspective for radical transformation of the entire profession is submitted here for consideration and future discourse.

Seven Pillars of Practice offers a new focus at the expense of defused and conflicted 'client-centred' approach. Mission, education and service—constructs of change in the whole HSD process—are unified in the buoyancy of authenticity, empathy and praxis that help achieve happiness and well-being in troubled time. In other words, people live metaphors of peace and prosperity without a Faustian bargain in the predatory culture.

I make a modest attempt to humanize knowledge, science and services to ward off the inevitable ravages of alienation, anger and anxiety. I believe true altruism is only attainable when SW becomes the end of itself. Contemporary SW, a mirror rather than a flame, is fraught with fallacies of *help* and *fake hope*. What we need are unpretentious angels of self-transformation.

Human destiny is entrapped in the conflicts of its own success.

There is light seed grain inside.
You fill it with yourself, or it dies.
I'm caught in this curling energy! Your hair!
Whoever's calm and sensible is insane!

—Rumi, *Open Secret* (667).

Afterword

The Truth is always naked. Any attempt to cover it is a lie. We live in a post-truth era where contradictions define identity. The ambiguity of real and unreal is an absurd phenomenon, which we are dealing with. This schizoid reality is the new foundation of a 'helping profession'. If mental health is a critical element—as Speaker Paul Ryan and his ilk believe[1]—the response (see what people think about the carnage[2]) to the Las Vegas gunman is an exemplar. In the post-truth culture, counter-factual reality becomes a dangerous chimera.

'Alt' is the new word for white supremacists in America. Violence erupted like a dormant volcano on a university campus in Charlottesville, VA, after a neo-Nazi protest erupted into civil rights mayhem.[3] President Trump invented 'Alt Left' as an amoral reality. Liberty, equality and freedom are noble values for a free society. However, persistence of bigotry, racism and xenophobia make a mockery of the world's leading democracy.

How to be free in an unfree world? That is the question that intellectuals in universities and colleges must teach. A few social programmes supported by mediocre state jobs and a locally endowed professoriate will not transform academia. SW's future rests on its standing amongst the cognate disciplines. The current self-exclusion

[1] Banality of crime and carnage, howsoever evil it may be, cannot be passed as a mental health issue. https://www.cbsnews.com/news/paul-ryan-says-mental-health-reform-is-critical-ingredient-in-stopping-mass-shootings/ (accessed on 5 October 2017). It is a dangerously political ideology. Social workers ought to refute and protest against this unforgivable naïveté. However, this will not happen in a therapeutic climate.

[2] It is instructive to know about this man and his mind. Public response will shape policy formulations. https://www.yahoo.com/news/will-happen-las-vegas-shooters-room-mandalay-bay-150549171.html (accessed on 5 October 2017).

in the name of autonomy and professional identity is a convenient untruth.

Small things bring big changes. Little changes—ideas, experiences and events of no general importance—can become tsunamis of transformation. Malcolm Gladwell (2000) made a theory of this butterfly-hurricane impact, if I may. It seems SW's *tipping point* that reached around the 1960s came and passed. In the post-globalized world, however, the 'tipping point' logic perversely follows the same principle. SW devolution in the age of robotics is a monumental event in the unfolding drama of human evolution.

Therefore we must make ourselves historical against a mystifying history, that is, historialize ourselves against historicity.

—Sartre 1992: 80

Bibliography

Andersen, Kurt. 2017. *Fantasyland: How America Went Haywire: A 500-Year History.* New York, NY: Random House.

Aronson, Elliot. 1999. *The Social Animal.* New York, NY: Worth Publishers.

Aspalter, Christian. 2006. 'New developments in the theory of comparative social policy.' *Journal of Comparative Social Welfare* 22(1): 3–22.

Ayers, Ian. 2007. *Super Crunchers: Why Thinking-by-Numbers Is the New Way to Be Smart.* New York, NY: Bantam Books.

Backman, Carl W., and Paul F. Secord, eds. 1966 *Problems in Social Psychology: Selected Readings.* New York, NY: McGraw-Hill.

Baron, Reuben M., and Graziano, William G. 1991. *Psychology.* New York, NY: Holt, Rinehart and Winston.

BBC News. 'Who is Gurmeet Ram Rahim Singh?' 25 August 2017. Available from: http://www.bbc.com/news/world-asia-india-41047531 (accessed on 25 August 2017).

Brooks, David. 2011. *The Social Animal: The Hidden Sources of Love, Character, and Achievement.* New York, NY: Random House.

Becker, Ernest. 1968. *The Structure of Evil: An Essay on the Unification of the Science of Man.* New York, NY: The Free Press.

Becker, Ernest. 1974. 'The Discovery of the Science of Man'. In *Social Science and Social Welfare*, edited by John M. Romanyshyn, 7–32. New York, NY: Council on Social Work Education. Becker, Ernest, 1975. *Escape from Evil.* New York, NY: Free Press.

Bhadravaja, S. In Rig Veda 6.031.02. Available from: https://rigvedaanalysis.wordpress.com/the-rig-veda-a-historical-perspective/ (accessed on 24 May 2015).

Berger, Peter L. and Thomas Luckman. 1966. *The Social Construction of Reality: A Treatise in the Sociology of Knowledge.* Garden City, NY: Doubleday & Co.

Birnbaum, Norman. 1988. *The Radical Renewal: The Politics of Ideas in Modern America.* New York, NY: Pantheon Books.

Biswas, Soutik. 'Who killed Dr Malleshappa Kalburgi?' *BBC News.* 31 August 2015. Available from: http://www.bbc.com/news/world-asia-india-34105187?SThisFB (accessed on 5 September 2015).

Blumenthal, Sidney. 2016. 'Banner Season: My Name Is Thomas Jefferson and I Approve this Mudslinging'. *Smithsonian* 47, no. 8 (October): 38–39.

Bleyer, J. 2015. 'Good in Bed'. *Psychology Today* (October): 42–43.

Brown, Brené. 2010. *Gifts of Imperfection.* Center City, MN: Hazelden Publishing.

Brown, Norman O. 1959. *Life Against Death: The Psychoanalytic Meaning of History.* New York, NY: Viking.

Cairae, Harsh Mahaan. 2014. *An Aryan Journey* New Delhi: Rupa, 2014.

Carter, Jimmy. 2014. *A Call to Action: Women, Religion, Violence, and Power.* New York, NY: Simon & Schuster.

Carstensen, Laura L. 2015. 'The New Age of Much Older Age'. *Time* (23 February–2 March): 69–70.

Christian, Brian and Griffiths, Tom. 2016. *Algorithms to Live By.* New York, NY: Henry Holt & Co.

Coates, Ta-Nehisi. *We Were Eight Years in Power: An American Tragedy.* New York: One World Publishing, 2017.

Coelho, Paulo. 1998. *The Alchemist.* Translated by Clifford E. Landers. New York, NY: HarperOne.

Colby, Ira. 2014. 'Challenging Social Work Education's Urban Legends'. *Journal of Social Work Education* 50, no. 2: 206–219.

Crowell, Nate. '9 Life Lessons from Prince for Social Workers'. *Social Worker Success.* 29 April 2016. Available from: http://socialworkersuccess.com/prince-life-lessons/ (accessed on 12 August 2017).

Economist, The. 'Art of the Lie: Post-truth Politics in the Age of Social Media'. 10–16 September 2016, 17.

Edsall, Thomas. 2014. 'On Suzanne Mettler's *Degrees Inequality*'. *New York Review of Books*, LXI, 9: 3.

Epstein, William M. 2017. *The Masses are the Ruling Class: Policy Romanticism, Democratic Populism, and American Social Welfare.* New York, NY: Oxford University Press.

Estes, Richard J. 1984. 'Education for International Social Welfare and Research'. In *Education for International Social Welfare*, edited by D. Sanders and P. Pederson (a joint publication of Council of Social Work Education and the Hawaii School of Social Work). Alexandria, VA: CSWE.

Deleuze, G., and F. Guattari. 1987. *A Thousand Plateaus: Capitalism and Schizophrenia.* Translated by Brian Massumi. Minneapolis, MN: University of Minnesota Press.

Diesing, Paul. 1982. *Science and Ideology in the Policy Sciences.* New York, NY: Aldine Publishing Co.

Diesing, Paul. 1991. *How Does Social Science Work?* Pittsburg, PA: The University of Pittsburg Press.

Douzinas, Costas. 2000. *The End of Human Rights: Critical Legal Thought at the Turn of the Century.* Portland, OR: Hart Publishing.

Douzinas, Costas. 2007. *Human Rights and Empire: The Political Philosophy of Cosmopolitanism.* Abingdon: Routledge-Chevendistt.

Feld, Shiela, and Norma Radin. 1982. *Social Psychology for Social Work and Mental Health Professions.* New York, NY: Columbia University Press.

Ferry, Luc. 2003. *A Brief History of Truth: A Philosophical Guide to Living.* Translated by Theo Cuffe. New York, NY: Harper Perennial.

Foucault, Michel. 1965 [1988]. *Madness and Civilization: A History of Insanity in the Age of Reason.* Translated by Richard Howard. New York, NY: Vintage Books.

Foucault, Michel. [1969]1972. *The Archaeology of Knowledge and The Discourse on Language.* Translated by A.A.S. Smith. New York, NY: Barnes & Noble.

Foucault, Michel. 1970[1994]. *The Order of Things: An Archaeology of the Human Sciences.* Translated by Les Mots et les choses. New York, NY: Vintage Books.

Foucault, Michel. 1973[1994]. *The Birth of the Clinic: An Archaeology of Medical Perception.* Translated by A.M.S. Smith. New York, NY: Vintage Books.

Foucault, Michel. 1977[1995]. *Discipline and Punish: The Birth of the Prison.* Translated by A. Sheridan. New York, NY: Vintage Books.

Foucault, Michel. 2011. *Lectures on the Will to Know and Oedipal Knowledge.* New York, NY: Palgrave Macmillan.

Freud, Sigmund. 1961. *Civilization and Its Discontents.* New York, NY: W.W. Norton.

Fukuyama, Francis. 2014. 'On the Spoils of War'. *Stanford* (July/August): 42–43.

Gibeny, Bruce C. 'How the Boomers Destroyed Everything'. *The Boston Globe.* 20 February 2017. Available from: https://www.bostonglobe.com/ideas/2017/02/26/how-baby-boomers-destroyed-everything/lVB9eG5mATw3wxo6XmDZFL/story.html (accessed on 19 September 2017).

Gilbert, Neil. 2017. *Never Enough: Capitalism and the Progressive Spirit.* New York, NY: Oxford.

Gladwell, Malcolm. 2000. The Tipping Point. New York, NY: Little, Brown and Co.

Gore, Al. 2007. *The Assault on Reason.* New York, NY: Penguin Press.

Gouldner, Alvin W. 1970. *The Coming Crisis of Western Sociology.* New York, NY: Avon Books.

Gordon, Robert. 2016. *The Rise and Fall of American Growth.* New Jersey, NJ: Princeton University Press.

Gibbs, Nancy. 2013. 'The Choice. Person of the Year'. *Time* (December 23): 72.

Gidla, Sujatha. 2017. *Ants Amongst Elephants: Un Untouchable Family and the Making of Modern India.* New York, NY: Farrar, Straus and Giroux.

Gladwell, Malcolm. 2000. *The Tipping Point: How Little Things Can Make a Big Difference.* New York, NY: Little, Brown and Co.

Harari, Yuval N. 2015. *Sapiens: A Brief History of Humankind.* New York, NY: Harper.

Harari, Yuval N. 2017. *Homo Deus: A Brief History of Tomorrow.* New York, NY: Harper.

Harris, Sam. 2010. *The Moral Landscape: How Science Can Determine Human Values.* New York, NY: Free Press.

Hartley, Eugene L., and Ruth E. Hartley. 1961. *Fundamentals of Social Psychology.* New York, NY: Alfred A. Knopf.

Hayman, Ronald. 1987. *Sartre: A Life.* New York, NY: Simon & Schuster.

Hume, David. [1739]1961. *A Treatise of Human Nature: Being an Attempt to Introduce the Experimental Method of Reasoning into Moral Subjects.* New York, NY: Doubleday Dolphin Books.

Leigh Buchanan. 2015. 'No Time to Relax? These Gadgets Will Change That', *Inc.*, April: 62–63.

Ioannidis, Dr John. 'Metaphysicians—Combating Bad Science', *The Economist.* 15 March 2014: 74

International Social Work [Themed Issue: Migration] 60, no. 3 (May 2017) Available from: http://journals.sagepub.com/toc/iswb/60/3?utm_source=Adestra&utm_medium=email&utm_content=Read%20the%20anniversary%20issue&utm_campaign=7J0030&utm_term= (accessed on 7 July 2017).

Isenberg, Nancy. 2016. *White Trash: The 400-Year Untold History of Class in America.* New York, NY: Viking.

Kapur, Sonia. Review of *Trans-national Social Work Practice* (edited by Nalini J. Negi and Rich Furman) (New York, NY: Columbia University Press, 2010) in *Journal of Comparative Social Welfare* 27, no. 3 (2011): 270.

Karger, H., D. Stoesz, and E.C. Terry. 2010. *A Dream Deferred: How Social Work Lost Its Way and What Can be Done about.* Brunswick, NJ: Aldine Transaction Pub (republished by Taylor & Francis, 2017).

Keats, Russell. 1981. *The Politics of Social Theory: Habermas, Freud and the Critique of Positivism.* Chicago, IL: The University of Chicago Press.

Kolbert, Elizabeth. 2015. *The Sixth Extinction: An Unnatural History.* New York, NY: Picador, Henry Holt & Co.

Kolhatkar, Sheela. 2017. *Black Edge: Inside Information, Dirty Money, and the Quest to Bring Down the Most wanted Man on Wall Street.* New York, NY: Random House.

Kuhn, Thomas S. [1962]1996. *The Structure of Scientific Revolution.* Chicago, IL: University of Chicago Press.

Lindesmith, Alfred R., Anselm L. Strauss, and Norman K. Denzin. 1975. *Social Psychology.* Hinsdale, IL: Dryden Press.

Lindzey, Gardner, ed. 1954. *Handbook of Social Psychology: Theory and Method.* Cambridge, MA: Addison-Wesley Pub.

Luce, Edward. 2017. *The Retreat of Western Liberalism.* London: Little, Brown and Co.

McGuire, William J. 1999. *Constructing Social Psychology: Creative and Critical Processes.* New York, NY: Cambridge University Press.

Manual, Z.E. 2011. *Tell Me Something About Buddhism.* Charlottesville, VA: Hampton Roads Publishing.

Marcuse, Herbert. [1955]1966. *Eros and Civilization: A Philosophical Inquiry into Freud.* Boston, MA: Beacon Press.

Marcuse, Herbert. 1972. *Counter-Revolution and Revolt.* Boston, MA: Beacon Press.

Marx, Karl. 1913. *Capital: A Critique of Political Economy.* Chicago, IL: Charles H. Kerr.

Mettler, Suzanne. 2014. *Degrees of Inequality: How the Politics of Higher Education Sabotaged the American Dream.* New York, NY: Basic Books.

McCarthy, Julie. 'Vigilantes in India: Protecting Sacred Cows, Promoting A Hindu Way of Life'. *NPR.* 2 May 2017. Available from: https://www.npr.org/sections/parallels/2017/05/02/526426203/vigilantes-in-india-protecting-sacred-cows-promoting-a-hindu-way-of-life (accessed on 14 August 2017).

Mishra, Pankaj. 2017. *Age of Anger: A History of the Present.* New York, NY: Farrar, Straus and Giroux.

Mohan, Brij. 1973. *Social Psychiatry in India: A Treatise on the Mentally Ill.* Calcutta: Minerva.

Mohan, Brij, ed. 1985a. *New Horizons of Social Welfare and Policy.* Cambridge, MA: Schenkman.

Mohan, Brij, ed. 1985b. *Toward Comparative Social Welfare.* Cambridge, MA: Schenkman.

Mohan, B. 1988. *The Logic of Social Welfare: Conjectures and Formulations.* New York, NY: St. Martin's.

Mohan, Brij. 1992. *Global Development: Post-Material Values and Social Praxis.* New York, NY: Praeger.

Mohan, Brij. 1996. *Democracies of Unfreedom: The United States and India.* Westport, CT.

Mohan, Brij. 1999. *Unification of Social Work: Rethinking of Social Transformation.* Westport, CT: Praeger.

Mohan, Brij. 2002. *Social Work Revisited.* Philadelphia, PA: Xlibris (Random House).

Mohan, Brij. 2003. *Practice of Hope: Diversity, Discourse, and Discontent.* Philadelphia, PA: Xlibris (Random House).

Mohan, Brij. 2006. 'Unification of Science, Knowledge and Truth: A Post-empiricist Theory of Logical Humanism'. *International Journal of Contemporary Sociology* (Special Issue) 43 no. 2: 281–299.

Mohan, Brij. 2007. *Fallacies of Development: Crises of Human-Social Development.* New Delhi: Atlantic Publishers.

Mohan, Brij. 2011a. *Development, Poverty of Culture, and Social Policy.* New York, NY: Palgrave Macmillan.

Mohan, Brij. 2011b. 'Social Policy for Transformative Practice'. *Journal of Policy Practice* 10, no. 2: 95–107.

Mohan, B. 2011c. 'Rights, Responsibilities, and Renaissance: The Three Rs of Sustainable Development.' *Social Development Issues* 33, no. 3: 74–77.

Mohan, B. 2011d. *Journal of Social Work Education* 47, no. 3: 621.

Mohan, Brij. 2012. *Society and Social Justice: A Nexus in Review.* Bloomington, IN: iUniverse.

Mohan, Brij, ed. 2015. *Construction of Social Psychology.* Lisbon: The Science Press.

Mohan, Brij. 2015a. 'The Aryans of Eurasia'. *Asian Journal of Indigenous Studies* I, no. 1 (Fall): 31–35. http://www.ajis.info/wp-content/uploads/2015/05/03-Brij-Mohan.pdf (http://www.ajis.info/)

Mohan, Brij. 2015b. *Global Frontiers of Social Development Theory and Practice: Climate, Economy and Justice.* New York, NY: Palgrave Macmillan.

Mohan, Brij. 2016. 'Environment and Social Psychology: A Good Nexus'. *Environment and Social Psychology* I, no. 1: 3–12.

Mohan, Brij. 2017. *Kafka's Cave: An Academic Memoir.* Toronto: Scholar's Publishing (forthcoming).

More, Thomas. 1965. *Utopia.* London: Penguin Book.

Morris, Ian. 2013. *The Measure of Civilization: How Social Development Decides the Fate of Nations.* Princeton, NJ: Princeton University Press.

Nagel, Ernest. 1961. *The Structure of Science*. New York, NY: Routledge & Kegan Paul.

Ohlson, K. 2015. 'The Einstein of Love'. *Psychology Today* 48, no. 5 (October): 72–81.

Pais, Richard. 2012. *Perspectives on Social Development*. Jaipur: Rawat Publications.

Parker, Ian, ed. 1998. *Social Constructivism, Discourse, and Realism*. London: SAGE.

Payne, Malcolm. 2014. *Modern Social Work Theory*. Chicago: Leycem, 4th ed.

Picketty, Thomas. 2014. *Capital in the Twenty-First Century*. Translated by Arthur Goldhammer. Cambridge, MA: Harvard University Press.

Pinker, Steven. 2018. *Enlighten Now: The Case for Reason, Humanism. and Progress*. New York: Vikings.

Potts, Malcolm, and Thomas Hayden. 2008. *Sex and War: How Biology Explains Warfare and Terrorism and Offers a Path to a Safer World*. Dallas, TX: Benbella Books, Inc.

Putman, Robert. 2015. *Our Kids: American Dream in Crisis*. New York, NY: Simon & Schuster.

Ravets, Jerome. 1971. *Scientific Knowledge and Its Social Problems*. New York, NY: Oxford University Press.

Razvi, Sulaiman. 'Hinduism Exposed Obscenity in Vedas'. *Truth About Hinduism*. Available from: https://truthabouthinduism.wordpress.com/2014/05/15/there-is-indeed-obscenity-in-vedas/ (accessed on 4 December 2017).

Reeves, Richard. 2017. *Dream Hoarders: How the American Upper Middle Class Is Leaving Everyone Else in the Dust, Why That Is a Problem, and What to Do About It*. Washington, DC: Brookings Institution Press.

Robbins, Susan M. 2014. *Journal of Social Work Education* 50, no. 4: 2 (in press).

Rabinow, Paul. 1984. *The Foucault Reader*. New York, NY: Pantheon Books.

Romanyshyn, John M., ed. 1974. *Social Science and Social Welfare*. New York, NY: Council on Social Work Education.

Rorty, Richard. 1999. *Philosophy and Social Hope*. New York, NY: Penguin.

Roth, Phillip. 2014. 'My Life as a Writer'. http://www.nytimes.com/2014/03/16/books/review/my-life-as-a-writer.html (accessed on 31 March 14).

Roy, Arundhati. 2017. *The Ministry of Utmost Happiness*. New York, NY: Alfred A. Knopf.

Sanneh, Kelefa. 2017. 'The Limits of "Diversity"'. *The New Yorker* (9 October). Available from: https://www.newyorker.com/magazine/2017/10/09/the-limits-of-diversity (accessed on 21 February 2018).

Saval, Nikil. 2014. 'The Office and Its Ends'. *Harper's* 328 (April): 11.

Sharlet, Jeff. 2008. *The Family: The Secret Fundamentalism at the Heart of American Power.* New York, NY: Harper Perennial.

Sharman, Jon. 'Psychiatrists Tell Congress Donald Trump is "a clear and present danger" to the world'. *The Independent.* Available from: https://www.yahoo.com/news/psychiatrists-tell-congress-donald-trump-074136725.html (accessed on 4 December 2017).

Siwach, Sukhbir. 'Haryana Sweet Water Pools Fire Up Saraswati Revival'. *The Economic Times.* 19 May 2015. Available from: //economictimes.indiatimes.com/articleshow/47229565.cms?utm_source=contentofinterest &utm_medium=text&utm_campaign=cppst (accessed on 4 December 2017).

Stoesz, David. 2014. 'A Letter to the Editor'. *Journal of Social Work Education* 50, no. 2: 385.

Stone, Brad. 2017. *The Upstarts: How Uber, Airbnb, and the Killer Companies of the New Silicon Valley Are Changing the World.* New York, NY: Little, Brown and Co.

Szasz, Thomas. 2004. *Liberation by Oppression: A Comparative Study of Slavery and Psychiatry.* New Brunswick, NJ: Transaction Publishers.

Sartre, Jean-Paul. 1992. *Truth and Existence.* Translated by Adrian van den Hoven. Chicago, IL: The University of Chicago Press.

Schilpp, P.A., ed. 1952. *The Philosophy of Sarvepalli Radhakrishnan.* La Salle, IL: Open Court.

Serwer, Andy. 2014. 'Waiting for Datapocalypse'. *Fortune* 169, no. 3 (February 24): 8.

The New York Times. 2017. '477 Days. 521 Mass Shootings. Zero Action from Congress', 06 November. https://www.nytimes.com/interactive/2017/10/02/opinion/editorials/mass-shootings-congress.html?emc=edit_ty_20171003&nl=opinion-today&nlid=72603810&te=1&_r=0 (accessed on 3 October 2017).

Taplin, Jonathan. 2017. *Move Fast and Break Things: How Facebook, Google, and Amazon Cornered and Undermined Democracy.* New York, NY: Little, Brown and Co.

Taylor, Richard. 1970. *Good and Evil.* London: Macmillan.

The Economist. 2015. 'The Great Fall of China', 29 August–4 September.

Thompson, Derek. 2015. 'A World Without Work'. *The Atlantic* 316, no. 1 (July/August): 50–61.

Turner, Francis J. ed. 1996. *Social Work Treatment: Interlocking Theoretical Approaches.* New York: The Free Press.

Ugiagbe, Ernest Osas. 2014. 'Social Work is Context-bound: The Need for Indigenization of Social Work Practice in Nigeria'. *International Social*

Work, Published online before print 1 April 2014. doi: 10.1177/002087
2813515013, April 1, 2014 0020872813515013.

Weick, Ann. 1991. 'The Place of Science in Social Work'. *Journal of Sociology
and Social Work* XVIII, no. 4: 13–34. Special issue on philosophical issues
in social work.

Will, George. 2014. 'Accusations Bring Back 50 Years of Denial'. *The
Advocate,* March 23 (Sunday): 7B.

Will, George. 2016. 'The 'Quiet Catastrophe' of Men Not Working'. *The
Advocate* (Sunday, 9 October): 7B.

Wilson, Edward O. 2014. *The Meaning of Human Existence.* New York, NY:
Liveright Publishing.

Wood, Graeme. 2015. 'What ISIS Really Wants and How to Stop It'. *The
Atlantic* (March): 79–94.

Yaccino, Steven, and Dan Barry. 2014. 'Bullets, Blood and Then Cry of "Heil
Hitler"'. *The New York Times* (14 April).

Index

About the Author and the Foreword Writer

Author

Brij Mohan is Dean Emeritus, School of Social Work, Louisiana State University, USA. Having taught at Lucknow University for over a decade (1964–1975), he moved to the United States of America where he served at the University of Wisconsin and Louisiana State University. He is Founding Editor of the *Journal of Comparative Social Welfare* (now published as *Journal of International and Comparative Social Policy*). Professor Mohan has published many books and papers on issues ranging from existential social work to transformative social practice. He speaks and writes about the human condition with undying hope for the survival of family, community and the world at large.

Professor Mohan received his Master of Social Work degree from Agra University. He received his doctorate from Lucknow University and an Honorary Doctorate of Letters from M.K. Gandhi Kashi Vidyapith.

Foreword Writer

Peter Herrmann is currently a Fellow at Max Planck Institute for Social Law and Social Policy, Munich, Germany. His affiliations also include Department of Social Sciences, University of Eastern Finland, Finland, and Corvinus University, Budapest, Hungary. His specialization includes social policy, social economy, European integration and social policy, NGOs and methodology and philosophy of social science. Most recently, he has authored *Opening Views Against the Closure of the World* (2016).

By the Same Author

Global Frontiers of Social Development Theory and Practice: Economy, Climate and Justice. New York, NY: Palgrave Macmillan, 2015.

Construction of Social Psychology. Introduced and Edited. Lisbon: InScience Press and The World Institute of Advanced Research and Science (WIARS), 2015.

Transforming Social Work. Based on a keynote address delivered to the 3rd Indian National Congress of Social Work, 24–26 October 2015. Lucknow: Rapid Book Service. (ISBN 978-93-82462-59-0) http://esp.whioce.com/index.php/ESP/article/view/01006

Death of an Elephant (debut novella). Bloomington, IN: iUniverse, 2013 (Republished by Scholars Publishing, 2014; trans. in Hindi by Kamal Varma, 2017; trans. in Persian by Mina Taherifard, 2018; in process).

Society and Social Justice: A Nexus in Review. Bloomingdale, IN: iUniverse, 2012.

Development, Poverty of Culture and Social Policy. New York, NY: Palgrave Macmillan, 2011.

Fallacies of Development: Crisis of Human-Social Development. New Delhi: Atlantic Publisher, 2007.

Reinventing Social Work: The Metaphysics of Social Practice. Foreword by Thomas D. Watts. Lewiston, NY: The Edwin Mellen Press, 2005.

The Practice of Hope: Diversity, Discontent, and Discourse. Foreword by David G. Gil. Philadelphia, PA: Xlibris/Random, 2003.

Social Work Revisited. Foreword by Johan Landon and S. Zafar Hasan. Philadelphia, PA: Xlibris/Random, 2002.

Unification of Social Work: Rethinking Social transformation. Foreword by Leon H. Ginsberg. Westport, CT: Praeger, 1999.

Democracies of Unfreedom: The United States and India, Westport, CT: Praeger, 1996.

Eclipse of Freedom: The World of Oppression. Westport, CT: Praeger, 1993.

Global Development: Post-Material Values and Social Praxis. Foreword by David G. Gil. New York, NY: Praeger, 1992.

Glimpses of International and Comparative Social Welfare. Ed. Canberra, Australia: IFSED, 1989.

The Logic of Social Welfare: Conjectures and Formulations. New York, NY: St. Martin's; Brighton, England: Wheatsheaf, 1988. (Also translated into Korean.)

Denial of Existence: Essays on the Human Condition. Springfield, IL: Charles C. Thomas, 1987.

Toward Comparative Social Welfare. Ed. Cambridge, MA: Schenkman, 1985.

New Horizons in Social Welfare and Policy. Ed. Cambridge, MA: Schenkman, 1985.

Social Psychiatry in India: A Treatise on the Mentally Ill. Foreword by Milton Lebowitz. Calcutta: Minerva, 1973.

India's Social Problems: Analyzing Basic Issues. Foreword by S. Zafar Hasan. Allahabad: Indian International Publications, 1972.